THE GARDEN AND THE GHETTO

Jeff Deel

WestBow
PRESS
A DIVISION OF THOMAS NELSON

ISBN: 978-1-4497-3314-8 (e)
ISBN: 978-1-4497-3313-1 (sc)
ISBN: 978-1-4497-3315-5 (hc)

Library of Congress Control Number: 2011962021

WestBow Press books may be ordered through booksellers or by contacting:

WestBow Press
A Division of Thomas Nelson
1663 Liberty Drive
Bloomington, IN 47403
www.westbowpress.com
1-(866) 928-1240

Printed in the United States of America

WestBow Press rev. date: 12/22/2011

PROLOGUE

Every city has a neighborhood people want to avoid. Many times even the folks who live there wish they didn't. They'd be somewhere else if they had a choice. You know the neighborhood. It is usually characterized by houses that need paint, dirty streets and sidewalks, empty lots strewn with glass bottles and trash, liquor stores and little shops that advertise "We Accept Food Stamps." These neighborhoods are populated mostly by people living below the poverty level, and their reputations are usually contemptible.

Atlanta's version of the community described above is called "The Bluff." It is our version of the ghetto, our poster child for everything bad in the inner-city. In Georgia, our zip code boasts first place in a number of notorious categories: Violent crimes, illegal drug activity, single-parent households, high school dropouts, inmates in Georgia's jails and prisons and so on. But, sitting right in the middle of this pivot point of so much that is wrong is a lighthouse of hope, a place where the last, lost and least can run for protection and help. City of Refuge occupies nearly nine acres in the heart of Atlanta's worst neighborhood, with 210,000 square feet of space under roof.

In 2004, the ministry moved from its modest, traditional facility on 14th Street to the present location in "The Bluff." The warehouse backs up to a railroad track between Burbank and Chappel Road, a city block the Atlanta Journal recently described as "Atlanta's new problem child." At the time of the report, there had been three murders on the block in one year. A couple more have been added since then.

City of Refuge cooperates with city and county government to provide Eden Village, a transitional living program for previously homeless women and children. The center has capacity for 285 residents and provides such services as free child care, mental and physical health assessments and treatment, child support issues, open DFCS and legal cases, career training and job referrals. The Resource Center provides assistance for thousands of clients each year, such as food boxes, hygiene kits, computer and phone usage, help with rent and utility bills, and referrals for drug/alcohol rehabilitation. The 180 Degree Kitchen prepares and serves nearly 20,000 meals per month and operates a culinary training center and catering service. A full-service medical clinic provides free services to Eden Village residents and people from the community. The HEALing Center is staffed by top level medical professionals and addresses most physical and mental health cases, including dental services and many surgeries.

Of course, children are at the heart of it all. The after-school tutoring program is alive and well, and when it comes to Christmas there's "no child left behind." The "Back to School Bash" provides book bags and supplies to hundreds of inner-city kids, and summer camps keep them off the streets during times when they are not in school.

When The Mission congregation meets for worship, it is to celebrate all that has happened during the week. When the people sing praises and clap their hands, it is to rejoice that the chains of injustice have been loosed and the oppressed have been set free. They take the mandate of Isaiah 58 literally, and when they worship they do so with the satisfaction that they have shared their food with the hungry and provided shelter for the poor wanderer. Middle class suburbanites sit shoulder to shoulder with former drug addicts and prostitutes, and ex-convicts break bread with people who have never so much as smoked a cigarette. When they absorb the preaching and teaching of ministry leaders, it is so the following week they may be better equipped to carry out the instruction of Jesus concerning "the least of these," for service is the purest worship and produces the truest reflection of the Kingdom.

Each church has its mission, vision and assigned place, and each one should include elements of evangelism, exhortation and discipleship. In impoverished and problem-riddled communities such as "The Bluff," evangelism must have trusting relationships as a cornerstone, and the most effective way to establish trust is to meet practical needs. As one frail, sickly, homeless man said, "I might not hear your words if my stomach growls while you are talking."

Exhortation must be balanced by example. The Kingdom message proclaimed by Jesus is replete with challenges to reach out to people living on the margins, but his commissions are always preceded or followed by his own actions. His call to the disciples was to "come follow me." In other words, walk where I walk and do what I do. In the ghetto, people give very little consideration to what is *said* but take great account of what is *done*.

Discipleship is for the purpose of equipping disciples for service. It is not a matter of what one knows, but what he does with what he knows. At The Mission, this much we know: We are surrounded by people who are hurting, hungry and desperate. We have been placed here for a purpose, and our commitment to equipping disciples to meet the needs is relentless. We MUST go to the poor wanderer and bring him in, and we MUST train others to do the same.

The Mission is tucked behind intimidating wrought iron gates and fences, but its light is permeating the neighborhood and darkness is perpetually pushed out. Atlanta's worst neighborhood is changing. The "problem child" is getting a makeover. As a result of obedience to the Father's command, light is "breaking forth like the dawn" and our "night is becoming like the noonday" (see Isaiah 58). Obedience has a way of bringing renewal and restoration. Ghetto life was never the Father's intention for his children, and He has made a way for them to return to a Garden existence with Him. As one long-time citizen said to a group of corner drug dealers, "Y'all might as well move out 'cause Jesus is movin' in!"

Fourteen years of ministry in Atlanta have provided more stories than we can count, and it is time to share a few of them. Our list of colorful characters and outrageous situations is too long to mention them all, and many stories cannot be shared publicly. There are far too many sordid details that no Christian publisher would dare print, so we will keep those locked in our personal files and focus on a few that are acceptable for all eyes and ears.

At this point it is important to explain that some of the stories you will read on these pages do not have happy endings. Some of the friends we have known through the years did not ride off into the proverbial sunset, destined to live happily ever after in the fullness of all Father had for them. Some of them made terrible decisions that cost them everything, including their lives. The power of these stories lies in their ability to illustrate the contrast between good and bad decisions, and their resulting consequences. It is to reinforce one of the most important lessons in Scripture: "Whatever a man sows, that will he also reap" (Galatians 6:7). The stories are shared so individuals who read them can draw wisdom and counsel from them that will make a difference in their own lives.

Life is a series of decisions, and our decisions will lead us in one direction or another. Good decisions will bring about good results. Wise choices will lead us into places of Peace and rest where we can grow into the sons and daughters our Father intends us to be. Even though calamity may characterize the world around us, we can dwell in the Garden of His purpose and have immediate access to Him. Bad decisions will have the opposite effect. They will produce bad results that lead to a knowledge of things Father never wanted us to know. We will suffer pain and heartache and will become part of the calamity rather than abiding in His spiritual Garden. Bad seed produces a rotten crop.

My wife is a great cook and truly enjoys discovering new recipes and trying them out on me. In her opinion, there are four divine beings, not three – Father, Son, Holy Spirit and Paula Deen. Each recipe she tries has a perfect culinary product as its ultimate goal. Each ingredient carries huge significance, and no recipe can be approached without all ingredients presented in the exact measurement the recipe calls for. The results are usually mouth-watering.

This collection of stories, essays, poems and reflections is a recipe of words, sentences, paragraphs and chapters. There are many types of ingredients, but the goal is to enable the reader to understand how to live in a way that gives him or her access to Father's Peace, Power, Provision and Protection every day. There are stories of victory and stories of staggering defeat. In some cases, names have been changed to protect the innocent… and the guilty. The bottom line of each story is the same: There is hope for each of us that we can know Father's original intention for us, understand that it has not changed, and take steps that will lead us back to the Garden of His purpose. He wants to walk and talk with us like He did with His first kids. He desires that we take a fresh look at the rest of creation and realize our connection to it, so that we can move into a lifestyle of obedience and the earth's groaning can stop. And perhaps chief of all potential lessons from this work is that our Father desperately wants each man, woman, boy and girl to know that we are brothers and sisters, and that we have a tremendous obligation to one another. He wants us to change the world by our love and devotion to our worldwide family. He wants Light to dispel darkness, Love to replace hatred, Compassion to push out cynicism and Forgiveness to take the place of blame.

When you have finished reading, it is my prayer that you will be shaken to the core of your spirit and thereby motivated to find the Garden Father has for you. Secondly, it is my prayer that you will pass the book on to someone else so they can do the same.

Peace.

I Am Just a Shepherd Boy
Pastor Bruce's Story

And in that vicinity there were shepherds living [out under the open sky] in the field, watching [in shifts] over their flock by night. And behold an angel of the Lord stood by them, and the glory of the Lord flashed and shone all about them, and they were terribly frightened (Luke 2: 8&9 Amplified).

In 1997 Bruce Deel was working at a nice church in North Atlanta when the denomination sent him on an unusual ministry mission downtown. The assignment was to close the doors of a small struggling church and sell the property. It was a *job* given by people with spiritual authority, so he made the shift and began the task. Since it was only a few minutes drive to the church in the city from their home in Stone Mountain, Bruce and his wife, Rhonda, decided to maintain their residence and commute to work and church. Their daughters continued to attend the same schools, play in the same sports leagues and enjoy the same lifestyle. He wasn't expecting God to do anything phenomenal – he was just *working*.

The tasks were simple: Find a good real estate agent and list the property for sale, get the property ready to sell, continue to have services and ministry opportunities, all the while preparing the few remaining brethren for transition to other places of worship and ministry. Bruce never asked God to show up in miraculous ways or "flash" in the night sky of dying ministry. For the most part his head was down, not in a depressed, melancholic mode, but because the assignment was on earth, not in the clouds, and he was determined to remain faithful to the things to which he had been called. At sixteen he realized the call of God on his life, and most of the early years in ministry were founded on an expectation of miraculous moments (the youth group to explode into the hundreds, miracles of divine healing and deliverance, unexplainable provision to show up in the mailbox). However, by 1997 he had concluded that ministry is mostly just plain work. It's just getting up day after day and completing the tasks that are before you, simply remaining obedient to Kingdom assignments.

In the process of *working* at Midtown Mission for what everyone expected to be a short six months, Bruce began to see flashes of God's glory. He wasn't really looking for them; they just showed up in ways that one would never have expected. "I am really glad I never asked God to do things a certain way because He may have honored my request and I would have missed seeing Him do things His way" he declares. He was busy cleaning out junk, negotiating with potential buyers, and preparing sermons when a flash would occur. As flashes of God's glory usually do, they caught Bruce's attention, and he was very thankful for good things that were happening. But following each experience, he went back to *work*.

For example, during service one Sunday morning a young lady walked in the back of the sanctuary and took a seat. She listened intently and seemed moved by the worship environment. At the conclusion of the sermon, she came forward and asked for prayer. She confessed she was thirty-two years old and had been working as a prostitute for fourteen years. That morning she prayed and was born into the Kingdom of God, a flash of His glory that was easily recognizable and for which the brethren gave Him great praise. On Monday morning Bruce went back to work cleaning, negotiating and preparing.

The following Sunday the young lady returned and brought with her a fifty-five year old man she described as "formerly one of my paying customers." This time the service was interrupted before the sermon was finished. The man wanted prayer. Obviously, he was not aware of proper protocol for salvation: Wait until the sermon is finished and come forward when the call is given; rather, he was compelled by Holy Spirit and could not wait. Bruce's evaluation: "I am glad he responded to Father's plan rather than following our order, or we may have missed another flash of glory."

On Monday morning, Bruce went back to work.

When the six months was up, the supposed temporary Pastor concluded that one should not close a ministry and move on to the next assignment when so much flashing is going on. By that time the congregation of twenty folks had tripled and a vibrant after-school program for inner-city kids was happening in the basement. Volunteers were distributing meals to the poor from the church's small kitchen, and the beginnings of a clothing closet were starting to take shape. Bruce decided to incorporate an outreach arm of The Mission and call it City of Refuge.

Outsiders were taking an interest in what was happening on 14th Street and were driving to the city from their suburban homes (much like the Deel family) to be part of it. While they were still behind bars, inmates in

Atlanta's jails and prisons were hearing about "The Mission" and making their way to the church upon release. Bruce *worked* to help them find jobs and places to live. He *worked* in cooperation with recovery programs and transitional living facilities to provide felons with a fresh start. He *worked* to secure properties where men and women could reside and be part of discipleship efforts. The flashes continued in regular succession, and with each one a little more of God's glory was revealed.

Each morning Bruce rose from his bed and went to *work*. The tasks began to take on different shapes, and soon the initial assignments faded into oblivion as he plowed into the future with blind faith and great expectations. The growing clan cleaned, painted and worked on the roof of the old church building. They modified the basement to better accommodate groups of kids and homeless people for hot meals. One day Rhonda surprised him with an announcement. "If we are going to *work* in the city, I think we should *live* there." It was another flash, and before long they were emptying their comfortable house in beautiful Stone Mountain and moving into the old church building on 14th.

Living in the building gave the Pastor many more opportunities to *work*. It was about twenty-five steps from his third floor door to the office, not to mention the regular flow of needy people who came to the church asking for assistance. It seemed most of these people had little understanding of "regular hours of operation." There were countless interruptions of family dinners, movies or ball games, and peaceful nights of sleep. Bruce began to bring in staff persons to help, and each one was put to *work*. He never hired a soul whose job it was to pray that God would do something miraculous. No one was given the assignment to stand in the parking lot and gaze into the sky with an expectation that God's glory might be revealed. No job description included a mandate to simply believe God for miracles. Oh, they prayed and regularly asked Father for His guidance, and that He would snatch them back into line if they ventured down paths of self-sufficiency, but mostly they just *worked* very hard at being obedient to the things He has commanded all believers to do: Feed the hungry, give drink to the thirsty, clothe the naked, befriend prisoners, take care of widows and orphans, love other people as much as they loved themselves. They busied themselves with all that kind of weird stuff that requires a little extra effort and omits most of the things that characterize modern day churches. But the flashes continued to come. Crack addicts were set free from their addictions. Prostitutes were redeemed and started new lives. Homeless people emerged from under bridges and realized there was hope, and babies born into extremely chaotic situations were adopted by wonderful families. And with each flash a bit more of the glory of God was revealed. Following each glorious episode, he went back to *work*.

As the months turned into years Bruce was compelled by the knowledge that most of the people who came for assistance were coming from a section of the city just west of the 14th Street location. They came down Bankhead, Simpson, or Martin Luther King, across Northside Drive and into the heart of the city where they could find people with disposable dollars, as well as organizations in the business of helping the poor. They came in search of food, clothes, assistance with utility bills, birth certificates and identifications, help getting into recovery programs and a multitude of other things. He realized that, in many cases, the process could be shortened and the effort people were making to get to The Mission minimized if operations were moved nearer to them. In 2003 Bruce assigned a real estate guy the task of finding a suitable facility in "The Bluff." The neighborhood was the worst in the city for many reasons. It was the kind of community that needed a lot of help, like a child with special needs.

While Rick looked for property, Bruce continued to *work*. There were too many things to do to sit around hoping and dreaming. He had more than one "visionary" contact him who wished to meet and talk about what they would like to see God do. Inevitably, the busy leader of what was becoming a dynamic inner-city ministry found he had no time for such meetings. He was duly busy doing the things about which Father had already given instruction. In other words, he already knew the heart of God toward the poor; God was just waiting for people like Bruce to stop dreaming and start doing.

After a period of diligent searching, Rick returned with this discovery: Eight and a half acres on Simpson Road (now Joseph E. Boone Boulevard NW) with two warehouses totaling 210,000 square feet of space under roof. The property was surrounded by wrought iron fencing, complete with razor wire and an armed security guard at the gate. It was perfect! Bruce asked Rick to negotiate terms with the owner while the work continued at The Mission on 14th Street. Rick reported the asking price for the property was 1.6 million dollars. Bruce sent a counter-proposal: "We love the property and wish to have it, but we do not have any money." The owner rejected the offer.

Rejection has a way of stopping some people in their tracks. Often it is a weapon that kills dreams and destroys potential. Many people have been cheated out of their purpose by allowing rejection to stop them from *working* toward their goals, causing them to give up. Marvelous inventions remain dormant thoughts because gifted inventors have allowed rejection to govern their efforts. Cures for horrible diseases may have gone unrealized because of the effects of rejection, and potential champions have likely gone uncrowned because they could not find the wherewithal to fight through rejection. When Rick brought the news that the asking price was still 1.6 million, Bruce Deel just shrugged his shoulders and went back to *work*. There was too much to do to spend time whining. After all, who really expects someone to sell you something so valuable for... nothing!

As the *work* continued, conversations would occasionally arise about the property on Simpson and Bruce would ask Rick to check with the owner again to see if things may have changed. Each time the answer was the same – 1.6 million. A few months passed and things continued to thrive at The Mission. One day as he was in the middle of some mundane task, such as meeting with children's ministry workers about summer camps, or planning the next neighborhood Matthew Party, or fixing a window broken during the most recent burglary, Rick called with an unusual message. The owner's lawyer had called to schedule closing on the Simpson Road property. Confused, Bruce responded to Rick that there still was no money for the purchase and he was not prepared to go that deeply in debt. As if telling his Pastor the daily specials at the Silver Skillet, Rick replied, "They want to *give* you the property."

FLASH!

Like shepherds on a hillside "watching over their flock by night," Bruce Deel spends his days (and nights when necessary) making sure the details of his assignment are completed. Shepherds make sure the sheep stay within protected boundaries, insure water and grass are readily accessible, keep the campsite stocked and organized, move the sheep when the time is right, and perhaps conduct business involved with shepherding. In the account recorded in Luke 2, the shepherds were doing nothing more than faithfully performing the duties associated with their jobs when the Creator of the universe showed up in a flash of glory, giving them a personal invitation to be the first outsiders to view the newly arrived Messiah. They were just "watching over their flock by night."

Oh, you'd better believe they hooped and hollered and high-fived each other the day the staff found out Mr. Mimms was donating the property to City of Refuge. It was a miracle of divine proportions and there were many reasons to celebrate; however, by now you know what happened when the fervor died down – back to *work*, for now there was much more to do than before. The buildings were dark, dirty, cold and empty. The ministry team was faced with the tasks of moving an entire church to a new location, preparing the old building to sell and making plans for the new facilities. The donation was a tremendous blessing but it also created far more work than they had ever known. They closed in a section of the warehouse and built offices. Completion of two basketball courts in one section of the building, and a work-out gym in another, provided multi-purpose space. There was lots of grass to cut and a huge parking lot to maintain. The fence needed repairs and *everything* had to be cleaned. They had this enormous place, now what in the world were they going to do with it?!

Bruce acknowledges he really did not know what to do or how to do it. He just went to work every day and did the things that were before him to do. He went to his pasture and cared for the sheep. He fed and watered, provided protection and direction, kept the place stocked and organized, moved the people along with him (spiritually), as Holy Spirit led, and conducted the business of shepherding. He kept diligent watch over the given assignment, refusing to allow it to be manipulated or destroyed by figurative wolves and coyotes. He was keeping watch by day and night.

Not long after the basketball courts were completed, Bruce was contacted by officials from city government and asked if he would open a thirty bed cold weather shelter for homeless women. The city would secure funding if City of Refuge would provide the facility. Since he was under a mandate to care for the poor (as are all human beings), Bruce complied and late in 2003 he set up thirty beds in the north gym and began to provide warm accommodation and food to the last, lost and least. A little time passed and he was asked to expand the shelter to fifty beds. When winter evolved into spring, he was asked to keep the shelter open another month, then another, then two more, then year round. They expanded to eighty beds, fifty in the gym and thirty in another section of the building.

As the months passed, Bruce realized more and more that Father is so blessed by our obedience to His instruction that He reveals His heart mostly in the process of that obedience. In other words, people are much more likely to hear from Him and grow in understanding of His thoughts and ways when they are busy doing His work. Scripture is pretty clear on the things true sons and daughters of Yahweh are supposed to do. In Matthew 25, Jesus reveals the aforementioned list of actions on which we will ultimately be judged (feed the hungry, etc.), and indicates the ministry of such actions to the poor and destitute is equal to ministry to Him. In addition, He paints a very clear word picture of judgment when He declares that sons who do these things will spend eternity with Him, and those who do not obey this very important instruction will not be recognized in the end as part of the family.

There is very little glamour in service. Mostly, it amounts to putting one foot in front of the other and getting one's hands dirty. Bottom line – service is the truest form of worship, and nothing pleases Father more than the true worship of service. This is not a doctrinal declaration of salvation by works alone, but there is no doubt that true sons and daughters of God have a responsibility to the poor and needy, and to ignore them is to live in disobedience to some of the most important instructions He gives. It is good to pray and fast and beseech Father to show His plan and reveal His will. It is better to get up from prayer time and get busy doing the things He has already commanded His children to do. In the midst of *doing* He will reveal flashes of His glory and revelations of His will like we never imagined.

With eighty homeless women arriving every evening, there was always plenty to do. There were meals to prepare (in an eight by fourteen foot kitchen), linens to launder, bathrooms to clean and stock (women go through unbelievable amounts of tissue!), shopping to do, fights to break up, and on and on. Just when things seemed to settle into a nice routine, another call came from city government: "Would you be willing to add another fifty beds to the shelter operation?"

WHAT?! Of course not! Our enclosed space is full! Our kitchen is too small! We are short on staff! But...I mean...fifty more women who are sleeping on sidewalks, under bridges, or in abandoned houses and apartments, scraping and scrounging and suffering day after day, hoping someone will come along and help. Of course not! I mean, maybe we can do something. I mean, what if it was one of my daughters in that situation? I mean, OF COURSE WE WILL DO SOMETHING!

The place may have been full at the time, but something had to be done, so Bruce went to *work* to find options. He thought of a man who was once part of The Mission family, but who had left to organize his own ministry and was reaching out to homeless people. He had recently obtained a spacious building a few miles from City of Refuge, so Bruce approached him with a proposal: We will provide the money to get the place ready and purchase beds if you will take the ladies in and provide shelter and meals. His answer: OF COURSE! Fifty more women off the streets and placed in an environment of hope and healing. FLASH!

You've heard of the snowball effect. It is the ideal metaphor to describe City of Refuge operations for the past few years. In 2007 the 180 Degree kitchen and dining hall were built, a gorgeous commercial kitchen and hall that accommodate more than five hundred guests for meals. As the *work* continued, grants and gifts started to pour in to pay for it. FLASH, FLASH, FLASH! Completion of this section of the warehouse afforded the opportunity to realize the vision for a culinary training school for young adults, as well as a catering business. As well, the new kitchen made it much easier to prepare several thousand meals per month.

Before the 180 Degree Kitchen was complete, as Bruce was in the midst of answering questions offered by plumbers, electricians and painters, as he was ordering tables and chairs for the dining hall, as he was meeting with staff to formulate plans for its use, as he was *working,* another call came from city officials, this time with the biggest question yet. They asked if COR would build a transitional living center for homeless women and children. The center would provide forty-two individual living units with a capacity for one-hundred thirty-five individuals. The program would include a full range of social services, including free child care, mental and physical health assessments and treatment, career development and job networking, assistance with open legal, domestic violence and DFCS cases. At the end of the four month program, the mothers and their children would transition into independent housing. The city would provide funding (1.5 million dollars) to build the center in a forty thousand square foot section of our warehouse, and would provide enough social workers to do the job, at a budget of $300,000 per year to pay their salaries.

FLASH!

To be chosen is an indescribable honor. Fact is, the Father has special assignments for each of us and loves to reveal them as we remain obedient to His instruction. Our best ideas cannot compare to His simple plan. Our greatest efforts are nothing more than wasted energy if not exercised within the framework He designs. We may accomplish things that are applauded by men and may win fantastic awards and receive tremendous accolades, but without faith in Him our works are temporal and will fade away. He knows our hearts, and if we follow His simple plan with great expectancy that from time to time He will show up in flashes of glory, He most definitely will.

In December of 2008 City of Refuge opened Eden Village, A Redemptive Housing Program for women and children. Once again, the responsibilities of Pastor Bruce and his staff took on new elements and required more of them than ever before. He hired more staff people (150 people living on campus 24/7 required a few additional hands). They worked to implement the programs, set policies, maintain facilities, set schedules, order supplies, raise money, and the list goes on and on. They have great times of corporate celebration. There are lots of good reasons to sing, shout, dance and otherwise offer gratitude to our Father, but mostly they make sure their daily *work* is seasoned with thankfulness for the opportunity to serve in the Kingdom of God. Each time a flash of His glory interrupts the routine, they feel more privileged than ever.

Bruce Deel is just a shepherd boy, but one who has seen brilliant revelations of the Peace, Power, Provision and Protection of the Creator. "I can relate to those simple men who sat on a Judean hillside on a clear night and had their plans interrupted by messengers from on high. In response to the call, I have journeyed to a nondescript place where I found the Spirit of Christ in the normalcy of servanthood. The more I just do what He says, the more of his heart and mind He reveals" – Pastor Bruce.

No sooner had Eden Village opened its doors than the call came from city officials to build Eden II. This addition provided a hundred more beds for homeless women. FLASH! No sooner had it opened than the call came to build a full-service medical clinic that would serve the community, as well as overflow emergency room patients from Atlanta's notoriously over-crowded Grady Hospital. Clinic construction was completed in May, 2011. FLASH!

Well, there is a lot of work to do because tending sheep requires constant attention. Just as his eyes were beginning to regain focus from the most recent flash, someone from the Task Force for the Homeless called to ask if Pastor Bruce could find room for thirty more ladies and kids. The weather in Atlanta is turning cold and the city's Gateway Center is overcrowded. There are lots of folks sleeping on the floor and in chairs. "In a way, I feel like I have been to the stable one more time and leaned over and felt the breath of God on my cheek again. I have heard the angels sing in the star-laden night sky, and now I am on my way back to the hillside to make sure the most weak and vulnerable of God's creatures are not left unprotected."

What a privilege.

THE BEST OF BOTH WORLDS

Pastor Bruce sits in his leather chair and observes his visitor, a person he has known since the early days in the neighborhood. Since the ministry moved to The Bluff, thousands of people have walked through the gate, most of them nondescript and unmemorable, a couple hundred "regulars" that everybody knows, and a handful of totally unforgettable characters that are forever burned into his mental landscape. There is Amy, proud owner of the foulest mouth in the history of the human race. She holds records in several categories - number of profane words used in one sentence, number of City of Refuge staff persons victimized by her verbal assaults, number of times the one finger salute has been offered in a day, and so on. There is John whose typical attire involves orange gym shorts, purple t-shirt, cowboy boots and a ten gallon hat. When he talks, he sprays saliva and whatever else is in his mouth. It may be Doritos, chewing tobacco, beef jerky, or some other healthy treat. My personal favorite is Cheetos soaked in red Gatorade. John pretends to be totally deaf to get hand-outs on the street. His hearing is impaired, but he is not totally deaf.

And there is Greg, perhaps earth's only inhabitant to have received a concussion from an owl, and to have given the owl a concussion in return. I'm sure you want to know more.

Previously an avid deer hunter, Greg was walking through the woods on an autumn morning, heading to his deer stand in hopes of bagging the big buck. It felt good to be in the woods. The morning air was crisp and clean and Greg found respite in being alone in the wooded sanctuary. It was his quiet time with nature and his thoughts. Suddenly, something slammed into the side of his head, producing a blast of pain, then blackness. He was unconscious on the forest floor. Unsure how long he lay there, Greg finally awoke, and with head throbbing and vision blurred sat up and tried to clear his thoughts. He was pretty sure he had been shot by another hunter, so he frantically rubbed his throbbing head in search of blood. His search produced no results, only more confusion, but as he continued to clear the cobwebs, Greg became aware of a rustling noise and commotion nearby. It was difficult to see, especially in his condition and in the gray light of early morning, but momentarily he found the source. A huge owl, only a few feet away, was staggering and stumbling, getting to its feet only to fall over again. The realization became clear. The owl had flown into Greg's noggin, knocking them both silly. It's one of those stories a person just can't make up.

Yes, more than a dozen years in the inner-city has produced an abundance of interesting characters, some male, some female, and some lost in a strange realm between the two. Bruce's current visitor is one of the unforgettables. Russell is a fiftyish former male homosexual prostitute who bears the temperament of an old woman and the wit of Mark Twain. He prattles on, jumping from subject to subject, and Bruce tries sincerely to concentrate, but his mind keeps wandering back to his first ministry job as Youth and Associate Pastor at a clean, white suburban church.

How did I get here? The question is a staple in his thought patterns, a constant query in his satiric ministerial world. As the visitor rambles on about nursing home jobs, lost IDs and his need for granola, Bruce wonders how it ever got this crazy.

Back to the early days and thoughts of padded pews, hymn books and parishioners in their suit coats and ties and bright Sunday dresses. He remembers playing basketball in the parking lot with teenage boys, youth retreats in mountain lodges and lock-ins in the church fellowship hall.

How the heck did I get here?

Where Pastor Bruce sits is a long way from Sunday School at Indian Valley Church of God, where he sat as a child under the tutelage of Sister Elizabeth, a blessed saint with a bounce in her step and a bun on her head. It is quite a distance from church camp where all the kids were the same color and the worst crime was duct taping a nerd and depositing him on the director's door step. And it is so, so far from his first ministry position, where the priority list was topped by tithes and attendance, necessarily in that order.

The visitor is now on the subject of his most recent job loss, and how he could "keep a job if the res' o' dem folk would jus' ack right." He has worked at a dozen or more nursing facilities in the past five years, but in each new endeavor he encounters "folk who don't ack right." After each exodus, the demand for nurses has thus far presented new opportunities for employment, but the proverbial bridges will eventually all be burned.

As a matter of fact, the focus of his ranting today is his lack of success at locating gainful employment. "They always brag on my job performance" he declares. "Can't nobody say I don't do a good job, when I got a job. Can't nobody say dat. It's jus' dem folk always shinin' on me, an' dey don't know me, Pastor. How dey gonna git in my bidness when they don't even know me?"

Bruce remembers Thursdays on the links with his first ministry mentor and boss, a leather-lung preacher and avid golfer. He thinks about the long discussions they had about the pros and cons of their current ministry assignments: Brother Joe is a very supportive board member. Attendance and tithes are up fifteen percent from last month. Sister Peggy is a gossip who likes to talk about everything from choir selections to the length of services to the clothes and jewelry worn by the Pastor's wife. There was stained glass and burgundy carpet, classrooms with tiny plastic chairs of different colors and shelves filled with crayons, story books and Christian videos. There were weddings, funerals, baby dedications, revivals and "special" singings. There were dinners in the fellowship hall with tables crammed full of chicken, ham, vegetables, forty varieties of bread, macaroni salad and every kind of dessert imaginable. Bruce licks his lips, dreaming of chocolate éclair cake.

"Pastor Bruce, you ain't listenin' to me, is you?"

"Huh? Oh, uh, yes Russell. I'm listening. I was just thinking of a church where I used to work."

"I was axing if you think dey got any o' dem granola bars ova in da kitchen. Can you call Chef Diana an' axe her?"

"You can walk over to the kitchen when you leave here" Bruce replies.

"If Diana has any granola, I'm sure she will give you some." From chocolate éclair to granola, from there to here, well, it is quite a shift.

Russell shifts his weight and crosses his legs, his motions girlish and deliberate. He reaches into his backpack and shuffles through piles of disorganized papers, pamphlets, snack wrappers, miscellaneous pieces of clothing and other odds and ends. Finally, he settles on something near the bottom and excavates it. It is a small purse, pink with lavender trim.

He places it on his lap, and Pastor Bruce watches with humored sadness as Russell unzips the purse and fumbles inside. Bold lavender letters on the purse's pink face spell out *Hannah Montana,* and a picture of the popular young entertainer's smiling face shines brightly. Under the picture is written the theme from the Hannah Montana television show, "The Best of Both Worlds."

Thoughts race back and forth from clean, comfortable ministry in places where people share common lifestyles and interests to ministry in the ghetto where fifty year old male, homosexual prostitutes carrying Hannah Montana purses sit across from you and talk about granola and the most recent profanity-laced tirade that resulted in another phase of unemployment.

"Oh, but I ain't never been fired, Pastor Bruce" Russell announces proudly. "I always *quit.* Dey can't never say dey fired me. I ain't never been fired one time in all my jobs. I always *quit* 'em ever one!" It is true that Russell has never been fired, just asked to resign more times than one can count. His patients sing his praises, turn in glowing reports of his compassion and tenderness, compliment him regularly on thoroughness and professionalism. Russell just can't get along with his co-workers and bosses. He despises being told what to do and snaps when singled out or embarrassed. He is perpetually paranoid that someone is trying to harm him.

Bruce offers a retort to Russell's self-affirming proclamation: "Well, I'm not sure it makes much difference, Russell. Employers don't look favorably on candidates that bounce around from job to job and leave trails of destruction at each one. You are not building a very good resume'."

"I know," Russell replies, his tone becoming self-piteous. "But, I'll find another job. Dey's jobs out there." Confidence returns.

Thoughts of Sunday night "evangelistic" services, attended by approximately forty percent of the suburban congregation's membership, and rarely by anyone needing to be "evangelized," not in the traditional sense anyway. Brought back by Russell's return to the land of the melancholy. "What's wrong wid me, Pastor? I know it's me dat's the problem, but I don't know why I keep on like dis and all dis stuff keep happenin' ova and ova." His eyes moisten and shift to portraits on the wall of Bruce's daughters. The emotion is half real and half intended to draw from the well of Bruce's sympathy in hopes that some tangible response will follow (granola bars, bus fare, new shoes, a new pocket book). It's part of the hustle. Tears are often included in the arsenal of weapons skillfully employed by the professional hustler, and Russell is a professional.

Bruce is thinking about a whitewater rafting trip down the Ocoee River many years ago, and how one kid almost drowned when he was thrown from his raft and pinned underneath. What if the kid had died? It would likely have changed the course of everything in Bruce's life, and he would not be sitting across from Russell and Hannah Montana. Something inside makes him even more thankful the kid survived, for had the Pastor's steps not brought him to this neighborhood, Russell would probably be dead as well.

Russell Freeman was first molested at five years of age by his cousin, although he says he participated in the act freely because he wanted attention and thought it was something everyone did. The experience was ugly and confusing and instantaneously changed his personality and the course of his life. Childhood years were spent in turmoil. The adults in Russell's life spent their time drinking, fighting and getting wasted. When he was barely old enough to go to the bathroom alone, his grandmother furnished Russell with alcohol – told him it was "good for the worms." The nurture and care due every child was absent, and peace was an abstract concept that related to nations and wars but had little to do with everyday life. Russell's world was noisy and vulgar, and following the first molestation he became increasingly angry and confused about his sexuality. Russell concluded that he was actually a girl who had been mistakenly assigned a boy's body. He made no attempt to hide this belief; rather, he flaunted it publicly and dared anyone to challenge him. Gone were the days when a trusted relative had to manipulate an unsuspecting child into some horrible deed. Russell now looked for opportunities to give himself to perverts and miscreants, and by his late teens was making a living at it. By age twelve he was working full-time as a homosexual prostitute, posing as a woman and steadily shooting into his veins a combination of heroine, cocaine and methamphetamine.

High School was brutal, as it usually is for kids who demonstrate homosexual tendencies, and Russell retaliated by becoming more and more blatant and by fighting. He was slightly built but absolutely unafraid of conflict. His angry explosions became legendary, and soon the bullies learned to keep their distance. On more than occasion he flashed a shiny blade kept deftly hidden in the folds of his clothing, just to let them know the score. He could still hear the giggles and whispers, but few had the guts to confront him face to face. Giggles and whispers were not worthy of consideration. There were much bigger wars to wage.

Russell's entire adult life has been a chaotic collage of angry emotions, valleys of depression, faint glimmers of hope, nights of debauchery and days flecked with the night's dark and toxic fallout. As a young man he turned more and more to alcohol to numb the pain and dull the voices in his head. Somehow he completed training to become a nurse, hoping a career helping others might cause his own needs to dissipate. So far it hasn't worked. He moves from job to job, each time with renewed commitment and dedication, each time pledging to function with a spirit of humility and cooperation, but each time giving in to his hatred of authority and blowing up.

"Dem folk jus' don't ack right. If dey would jus' ack right I wouldn't get mad. Somebody always got to shine on me. Why folk got to shine on folk? Dey need to take you to the side and discuss things witcha and not be shinin' you out in front of other folk." The more he elaborates, the more intense Russell's tone becomes, but he suddenly turns somber again. "But I know it's my fault." Since he was five Russell has lived with the unfulfilled hope that people will "jus' ack right." But they never do.

Some readers will hastily agree with Russell's self-blame and conclude that he is a fifty year old man who is responsible for his own actions, and that his wrong choices are willful and controllable. Some will readily decide that Russell should lay down the bottle, clean himself up, renounce his homosexuality, get a good job and keep it, and go to church with Brother Joe and Sister Peggy every Sunday. Some will even scoff and offer their disdainful rebuttals. After all, homosexuality is an issue many Christians have little tolerance for, but those who offer cynicism and condemnation rather than understanding, grace and mercy have their own confusions and problems. Hopefully, the path they trod will eventually lead to deliverance as well.

Personal accountability notwithstanding, the fault begins with Eve, Adam, Cain, Russell's parents, grandparents and his cousin. Disobedience in the Garden by the Father's first children provided to Russell and all human beings knowledge of perversion and addiction they would otherwise

21

not possess. Cain's choice to ignore the Father's instruction to do what is right, and instead to formulate and follow his own ideas paved the way for darkness and chaos to characterize God's creation. People who conclude that guys like Russell should simply make a choice to rise up out of their circumstances and do better do not understand what happens in the mind of a child who is raped. Such an act is not just an unnatural physical assault. The mind and emotions are brutalized as well, and the effect is almost always life-long. It is like a child standing before a spotless mirror, viewing himself exactly as he is, when suddenly a person he knows and trusts, who is supposed to be there to nurture and support him, rushes up and strikes the mirror, sending cracks and splinters in every direction. The child now stands before the same mirror but can only see distorted, twisted, confusing bits of the former image. Before long he doesn't know who he is or why he is here.

In Russell's case the childhood trauma destroyed his innocence and robbed him of the wonder and tranquility that should characterize every child's life. Birthdays and Christmases came to mean nothing. Every relationship was tainted with the poison of manipulation and love became a dirty word. No one could be trusted, and in his mind everyone wanted something from him and he was going to get something in return. Russell has come to believe the act of sexual assault perpetrated by his cousin was consensual and was good because it helped him realize his identity at an early age. "I wanted it," he declares, "and I'm glad it happened."

In addition to the emotional and mental damage, the practical fallout of Russell's childhood experiences was devastating. Though strong and clever, he has lived fifty years in poverty, sometimes in dank, smelly apartments and other times under bridges or in the woods. Dependence on hand-outs from food pantries and churches is a way of life and he is not unfamiliar with the inside of a jail cell. He was once run over by a car driven by an enemy out for revenge. The incident nearly severed Russell's right leg and he still limps. His addictions ride his shoulders like vultures, their claws imbedded so deeply any recipe for freedom must include the word "miracle." Pray for a miracle.

People like Russell require re-creation. His body is broken and desecrated and his spirit fractured like the aforementioned mirror. Russell's mind has been inundated with noxious ideas and toxic lies for so long, the idea of clearing it out, cleaning it up and starting over is akin to dipping the ocean dry with a teaspoon and refilling it with fresh water. What he really needs is a new mind.

Bruce interlaces his fingers behind his head and watches Russell pack up his things and prepare to leave. "I got to get my bidness together so I can find me another job," Russell says. "So you think da Resource Center can help me get my ID? An' you think I can get some o' dem granola bars?"

"Go out and talk to Summaria about the ID" Bruce replies. "I'm sure she will help you...again."

"Yeah, I'll talk to Summaria, but I ain't talkin' to Seff, 'cause dat man ain't right. He don't wanna help nobody. Him and dat little shawt man dat stay in the dining hall on Tuesday and Thursday. He ain't right neither. I asked him to use his phone las' week 'cause it was rainin' and I needed a ride. It was cold and rainin' an' I had to walk two mile downtown an' he wouldn't let me make a phone call." Russell's tone is bitter and vengeful.

"I'm sure he had a good reason," Bruce says, knowing his words will be rejected before they land solidly on Russell's ear.

"Naw, he ain't had no good reason. He was jus' standin' there feelin' good about bein' able to tell me *no*. So, I jus' tol' him he don't know Jesus, so he might a well fake it 'til he make it. Him and Seff both. Dey might a well fake it 'til dey make it 'cause dey don't neither one of 'em know Jesus."

"I'm sorry, Russell. I will talk to them."

"What would Jesus do, Pastor Bruce? Dat's all I wanna know. What would Jesus do? Folk always up in my Kool-Aid and dey don't even know the flavor. I don't get dat. I jus' wanna know if dat's what Jesus would do. Wouldn't Jesus tell folk to mind dey own bidness? Ain't dat what he tol' dem scribes and Pharisees? Ain't dat the lesson he taught dem folk in the temple when he took dat whip and busted 'em up? Dat's what I wanna do sometime. I jus' wanna carry me a whip for da hypocrites. Dese folk talkin' 'bout Jesus and won't even let folk use dey phone. What would Jesus do?"

Bruce fights back a smile at the thought of Russell brandishing a whip and giving Matt a lesson in what Jesus would do. He gathers himself and replies, "Well, we can't always do what Jesus would do, Russell. He would probably heal you, deliver you from your addiction and set you free in an instant, and I wish He would. But that's up to Him. We can't always do what He would do; we can only do what He has told us to do."

"So, what did Jesus tell dat little man to do, tell me to walk two mile in the rain?"

"No. My guess is Matt was probably busy with Safe Haven because he had a couple dozen volunteers to coordinate and a couple hundred people to feed. I'm sure he would have assisted you when the time was right. Maybe he doesn't know you like I do and know that you can be trusted. Maybe he's only thinking about the number of times workers here have loaned out their phones only to have them walk out the gate."

"I still say he might a well fake it 'til he make it. I don't know why he got to shine on me. He can call me to the side and esplain things. He ain't got to shine me out. Anyways, what is it Jesus tell y'all to do den?"

"He tells us to feed the hungry, give drink to the thirsty, befriend strangers, clothe the naked, care for the sick and visit prisoners. He tells us to provide the poor wanderer with shelter and to not turn our backs away from our brothers and sisters. Now go and get your granola bars."

Russell has no more arguments. He knows his Pastor is right. This man and his City of Refuge have been in this neighborhood more than a dozen years doing what he just described. The mandate is clear: Build a house with rooms for people like Russell, a place where the last, lost and least can come for healing and renewal, a place where the old mind can be traded for a new one, a place where re-birth is really possible. With God, it is even conceivable to dip the ocean dry and re-fill it with fresh water. With Russell, it's one spoonful at a time.

The visitor tucks Hannah Montana into his backpack and shuffles out of Bruce's office. He will visit again soon. After all, he is one of the "regulars," and he is family. When Sunday arrives he will occupy his spot in the place of worship, hands lifted high or clapping with great energy, praising the One who is leading him from the valley of the shadow of death into the Garden of his Purpose. He has been sober for fourteen months and is living in a City of Refuge transitional home. Although there is still a long path to travel, there are plenty of reasons to celebrate.

Bruce leans back in his leather chair and contemplates "the best of both worlds."

I'll take this one he concludes.

THE GARDEN

Eve awakes on a carpet of perfectly manicured grass and immediately is overtaken by the morning's smells. She closes her mouth and inhales deeply, processing and separating the combinations – rich honeysuckle, luscious pear, something... buttery. There is clarity of thought and perception that allows the smells to temper Eve's mood, to put her at perfect ease in her world. Though the night's sleep was flawless and uninterrupted, the morning's breath brings fresh relaxation and tranquility.

She ties her long, silky hair into a thick braid, all the while drawing in more deep breaths and reveling in the intoxicating smells. *There* she thinks *is rhododendron, and* she pauses, *I think that is cantaloupe. Adam must be cutting cantaloupe.* She smiles and decides to walk.

Eve is postured like an athlete with every muscle to exact specification for perfect mobility, every joint and ligament exquisitely attached and lubricated. Every cell of Eve's body is perfectly hydrated, and her organs function with more precision than intricate time pieces that will one day be invented by geniuses. When Father fashioned in His mind His first daughter, He smiled. Before dust was gathered and the artistry began, somewhere on a sacred spot on the earth's floor, Father's heart swelled at the thought of what He was about to create. He thought of Adam and the anticipated reaction to his forthcoming life partner. Out of His own loving heart and in His image, Father had made this man, and He knew the emotional connection between man and woman would be immediate and profound.

There is a section of the Garden she hasn't visited in a few days, a place where song birds congregate and put on morning concerts. Eve loves this part of her world, for it seems the birds react to her presence, intentionally fluttering to make their presence known and increasing their musical efforts just for her. She feels like a princess for whom a meticulous and spotless environment has been created. The birds are making new music this morning, melodies never before composed, harmonic colors never before painted.

Eve slows her gait to catch it all, moving through trees and past flower gardens and vegetable patches that brim with color and quantity. The birds sing about these trees and colors and provisions. They sing about Eve as well, and their song, like its subject, is perfect.

She spends a dazzling morning by the sparkling river that cuts through the Garden's eastern corner, watching trout the length of her arm glide by in their watery world, stroking the feathers of a magnificent eagle perched majestically on a low limb, preparing a story book picnic spot for dinner with Adam. She swims for a while, her elegant figure cutting effortlessly through the clear water. As she walks back onto dry land, a warm breeze blows up from the south and dries her off in moments, leaving her feeling cleansed and complete.

The day absolves itself of the constraints of time. There are no deadlines to create stress or pressure, no reason to look back or before, no regret, no consideration of disavowals, no fear of failure. There is only perfect satisfaction in each moment and the absolute attestation to the Father's faithfulness. Affliction is a word not yet assembled, conflict an idea not yet systematized, confusion a plague not yet launched, rejection a theme for future generations. Shame remains a concept as foreign as dust particles on a distant planet, and lust as removed as galaxies afar. War? There is no definition for ideas not yet formulated. Here there is only love, devotion and tranquility.

Eve relaxes under a splendid shade tree and watches her husband approach from across the meadow. *He walks like Father* she thinks. *He is gentle but strong, casual but purposeful, tender but aspiring.* Adam carries a basket laden with rose petals – red, yellow, white and pink - and as he comes nearer he begins to toss them by the handful into the air, watching them flutter to the ground like so many gorgeous butterflies. Some land in her hair and on her body but most on the ground at the base of the tree, their unmistakable scent permeating the air. She laughs and reclines, feeling the cool softness of the petals on her skin. *He thinks like Father, too – selfless and caring, passionate and attentive, wholly devoted to me.*

They eat a spectacular meal highlighted by three savory vegetables sampled for the first time. There is always something new and it seems each meal is better than the one before. They talk of the animals and the pure joy of getting to know them. They laugh about the little furry one with the bugged eyes they just discovered the previous day. Just as they finish dinner, they hear the familiar voice of their Father calling their names and laughing loudly. They look to the left and right, ahead and behind, for it seems He speaks from everywhere. It seems his laughter rises up out of the trees and floats by on the water. Simultaneously, He comes down from the sky and up from the earth, converging from the east and west, gathering like billowing clouds from the north and south. He emerges from the trees and makes His entrance from each blade of grass. His laughter fills the Garden, His sound, scent and breath lifting nature to her pinnacle.

And He is there, laughing and pointing at the rose petals, gently picking one from Eve's hair. He hugs them and touches their faces, then says resolutely, "Let's walk." Their walks amount to exploration – seeing new groves and rivers, discovering new animals and giving them names. Today Father takes them to a flower garden surrounded by magnificent trees, the leaves of which are brilliant shades of purple, yellow and orange, not gaudy and fluorescent, but deep and pure. Father talks to them about trees and their place in creation. He explains how trees stand as symbols of their own life experience and how they reach to the heavens in acts of purely selfless worship. He notes how their roots are one with the earth and how they emanate life and make everything else more alive. He points out the beauty and elegance they bring to the landscape. They move from tree to tree, noting the uniqueness of each one, the diversity of style, stance and color.

The tone of Father's voice massages the spirits of His children and His instruction bears the temper of a kind teacher. "I have a surprise for you" He declares, a smile hanging on the corners of His mouth. "I want to show you where it began. You should cherish what you are about to see, for it is the truest representation of Me that you will discover in this place. If you cannot find Me, make your way here and be reminded I have made a way to sustain you. It is the Garden's original implement; it is the essence of all that is."

As He finishes the sentence, the three of them step into a clearing and before them are two trees that rise in majesty above everything else. Eve and Adam stand speechless, unable to formulate language or perpetuate emotion in response to what they see. The trees are enormous in size and bear an aura that reminds them of the Creator standing beside them. They have witnessed breathtaking trees in other parts of the Garden, trees that shade half an acre of space, trees that house thousands of song birds and hang heavy with luscious fruit. But these trees are grandfathers, and they embody all the elements of every other tree in the Garden. All others are born of these two, it seems, each with traits of its ancestors, but none with full pedigree.

"This is where it started" Father explains. He looks at Adam and continues, "When I made you, I knew I must make a place for you. First I made a tree, for I knew the right tree would provide you shelter, sustenance and satisfaction. I poured Myself into the tree so you would always know where to find Me. I walk with you in the cool of the evening, but you may find Me any time. The tree is Life and in it is everything you need. In it you will find Me, for I am Life." Father walks to the tree on the right and places His hand on its trunk. A cool breeze stirs and the leaves overhead rustle. The limbs are laden with fat fruits of different shapes, sizes and colors. The breeze arouses aromas that make their mouths water.

"May we?" Eve asks. Father smiles, reaches up and plucks a handful of fruit and gives it to them. They simultaneously smell their respective portion and extend it to the mouth of the other, a practice they began on their first day together. The bite is exquisite, easily the best thing they have yet tasted and seems to have an effect that surpasses physical sustenance. It arouses spiritual energy and makes thoughts crystal clear and the connection to Father more intrinsic than ever. His expression pronounces His satisfaction and He quietly declares, "It is good. It is very, very good."

"Life is all you need" He states matter-of-factly. "It is My greatest gift to you. It was in My heart before the foundation of the world, and I chose to form you in My image and give you My life. Life is not your choice, it is My choice. I created you and I created this tree *for* you. The rest of your home was built around the tree, for this is the center of everything." The children listen intently, absorbing the Father's words and feeling full of the Life of which He speaks. They sit on low hanging limbs and learn of Him, reveling in His stories of calling Light out of darkness and order from chaos. They are awed by His lessons in architecture and how He formed everything they see from nothing but His own idea, and how everything He formed symbolizes some part of His character or some attribute of His nature. The flowers portray the beauty of His heart toward His children, flawless in its intention and presentation. The water in the

Garden's lakes, rivers and streams signifies the purity of His purpose. The mountains they can see in the distance represent His power and mystery, elements He explains no human being will ever fully understand. The breeze connotes peace and the vegetation His unfailing provision. The trees are His protection for they are strong and indomitable.

Eve hops down from her perch and gives Father an enormous hug. Over His shoulder she can see the massive twin to the tree under which they stand, its canopy painting the afternoon sky and its limbs laden with colorful fruits as well. Father is giving a lesson on the Lights of day and night, but Eve's attention is on the other tree and she wants to run to it and share her devotion. She wants to give equal attention to everything Father has created, to learn all she can about the design and purpose of all she sees. As she studies the second tree's broad reach, colossal trunk and abundance of fruit, Father's words become lost in the current of her own thoughts. She wonders if its provision affords the same Life as the first, wonders why Father focuses on one tree and leaves the other to stand unattended, debates whether or not to ask. Eve relaxes the hug and kisses Father's cheek, but her eyes never leave their target.

Adam watches his mate with fantastic curiosity. He is regularly amused by the fascination he sees in her eyes and the energy created by it. She is full of questions and is much more inclined to ask them than he is. Adam is patient and perceives that Father will reveal everything He wants them to know in His own time and by His own methods, but Eve is eager and excitable. Together they make a good pair. Adam suspects she wants to know about the other tree and is filtering ideas when Father speaks.

"That one is for Me." His tone is relaxed but resolute, and the children turn to see Him facing the other direction, staring toward the woods they walked through to get to this spot.

"But, what is it for?" Eve inquires, her mood still bearing the excitement of the day. "It looks like the other one. The fruit is the same. The leaves are identical and the limbs are low and easy to climb, just like this one." As the last words escape her lips a whisper runs across Eve's ear. It is a fleeting touch of breath, like a moth's wing or the brush of a feather. She barely notices it, though the thought runs through her mind that another brand new piece of this life is in process of revelation.

"It is for Me" Father repeats. He turns back to them and walks again toward the tree of Life. He extends His hand and strokes the lines on its trunk, a potter tenderly analyzing the finished product, a sculptor scrutinizing the polished piece. "Here stands a masterpiece" He says. "If it was the only tree I made, it would be enough. It is Life and it is all you need. You may come to this tree as often as you like. You may climb its branches and eat its provision. You may relax in its shade as you sit with each other and with Me and sort out the mysteries of the Spirit who hovers over your Garden home. And all the rest is yours, created for your pleasure and sustenance, but *that* tree is for Me." He still does not look toward the second tree but continues to speak of it as though it demands solitary consideration. He tells the children that the fruit of the second tree bears knowledge that is His alone to absorb and assimilate. He explains that their minds are not capable of managing the things the tree would present and that the enlightenment it could bring will destroy them.

Father turns to find Eve and Adam gathered closely behind Him, Adam's arm around her shoulder and the two of them listening intently. Father steps to them and wraps His arms around them both and it feels as though they are inside His heart, waiting once again to be born. They are close enough to feel His heartbeat and realize simultaneously that their hearts are beating in perfect synchronicity with His. Without speaking He gives them His thoughts and love, and they understand. He whispers, "Listen, there is nothing you need to know except Me and what I reveal to you. You cannot manage spiritual contrasts – that is a task for Me alone. I know you do not understand what I am saying to you, but you do not need to understand. Trust in Me and the plan I have for you. There are many, many things that must remain secret. If they are revealed, the earth will shift and become angry, and you will be forced to fight for your survival and will spend your days looking for Me and longing for what you had. Ultimately, you will die."

Adam studies Eve's face, wondering if his thoughts and questions are hers as well. *Angry...fight...survival...DIE...* – these are new words that carry a discordant tone, and he doesn't like them. The idea of "looking for" Father seems foreign and silly, and how can they possibly lose what they have? *This is all there is* Adam thinks, *or is it?*

Father turns and moves across the meadow toward the river, His children at His side and His powerful arms around their shoulders. They sense His pure devotion and are content in His presence. In the deep recesses of their individual spirits, each of them knows He is constant and unfailing. The evidence of His devotion is all around, and the security it produces is as natural a part of their existence as breathing.

The afternoon melts into evening and Eve and Adam lie on their backs and watch the sun disappear beyond the western fringe of the Garden. They know nothing of time save the rising and setting of the glorious Day Light. Before she falls asleep in Adam's arms, Eve contemplates all she has experienced in this place, a caring Father who adores her, a loving husband and soul-mate, a perfect life in a perfect place. But her thoughts drift to the center of the garden and two trees that stand above the rest. She considers them both but is soon drawn in by the mystery of the one on the left, the one called Knowledge.

From the day of her introduction to two essential trees in the center of the Garden, every morning Eve strolls through her sanctuary to that same spot and worships at the tree of Life. She sings songs and roams through its grand network of limbs and leaves. She partakes of the fruits, a deep green orb with the texture of silk, a canary yellow combination of sweet and sour juices with meat that brings potent energy, little bunches of blue-purple delight. She loves this tree more and more as she recalls Father's words and understands His counsel. Occasionally, Adam comes with her, but both enjoy individual worship and learning experiences as well. Eve loves her husband but also treasures solitude and revels in the idea that she can learn things on her own and bring them to Adam as revelation.

Morning by morning she comes to the clearing and stands before the two trees. Although the principal time is given to the tree on the right, each morning she pauses to examine its counterpart and to remember Father's words, "That one is for Me." She tries to distinguish between the two towering works of Providence but fails in her efforts. Sometimes Eve thinks she hears a quiet voice as she contemplates the mystery, much like the whisper that came during the first visit, and the resonance makes her uneasy. At first she looks around for Adam or Father, but she knows it isn't them for their voices are as familiar as her own, and they have no reason to whisper. Eventually, the whispering gains strength and the words clarity until Eve begins to make them out – *knowledge…power…strength…you…,* and she is captivated by the riddle of the tree and the enigmatic voice that brings it to her. Day by day she listens more intently - *self… discernment… perception… equality… rights,* and the words begin to produce boldness and confidence that there is more she should know, and that there are no limitations on what she can do with that knowledge. The voice becomes louder and more intriguing, demanding her ear and thought, causing her to forget Father's words and to justify the shift in her loyalties and allegiance of time. Day by day Eve gives a little more attention to the tree on the left and a little less to her original place of devotion.

As time passes and the couple dwells in the meticulous harmony of Garden life, everything becomes more familiar and Eve becomes more dedicated to understanding the mystery of the tree of Knowledge. She begins to repeat the words she hears in hopes they may come together to form an answer. The result is not revelation; rather, the practice seems to open doors for more questions. In addition to a steadily increasing file of words with which she is not familiar, she begins to see flashes of startling scenes and hear alarming noises she cannot explain, and they disturb her dreams – a faraway wailing accompanied by explosions of harsh red light against a black backdrop – a crimson puddle of liquid spreading across a rough gray surface – the silhouette of a body falling from a cliff to rocks below.

Many times Eve wants to run from the meadow and find Father. She thinks she should ask again about the tree, but He has explained and offers nothing more. She thinks of discontinuing solitary visits, but in the end the thrill of discovery and the challenge of detection push her on and she begins to climb and play on the tree's branches, completely unaware of the serpent that watches from the tree's highest limb. The serpent has been there the whole time, watching as Eve comes to the meadow each morning and formulating a plan for her demise. It is his deceptive voice that sends to Eve words she has never heard and draws pictures she has never seen. His cunning is diabolical and his methods ruthless. He gives no credence to time or circumstance. He patiently implements his strategy and works his scheme. Slowly the serpent turns Eve's mind and devotion toward herself, away from the neighboring tree and her adoring Father. He cares not if she trusts his voice. He only desires that she believe in herself more than she believes in Father. He comes to her on a lucid morning and helps her solve the riddle: "If you eat of this fruit, you will not die; rather, you will know what Father knows and you will be more like Him. You will have His knowledge, power and strength. You will possess the ability of discernment and perception and will no longer have to depend on Him for everything. You can make your own way, have equality with Father, exercise the full rights of divinity. What can possibly be wrong with that?" The serpent declares proudly, "I live on the fruit of this tree; believe me, Father will be proud that you acted independently and can now take your rightful place. You have the ability to create and govern. The fruit will simply bring revelation and disclose the pathway to your own deity. How do you think I got here? If this was something destructive, do you think Father would have shown it to you? Why would He not protect you from it altogether and keep it hidden?"

Eve listens and finds it difficult to process the serpent's words. She is not familiar with much of the language. Words like *wrong, destructive, protect, hidden* are confusing, but perhaps learning these concepts is part of the revelation. She is compelled to know more and enthralled by the idea of working with Father to create and govern.

With her hands full, Eve turns to leave the meadow, noting the darkness that looms to the west. She does not recognize the emotion stirring in her chest, that brings water to her eyes, and she has no idea how to react to it. Her breath catches in her throat as she nears the other tree and sees Adam standing next to it. She calls his name but the effort seems to echo back to her without effect. He stands and waits as she makes her way to him. He takes some of the fruit from her hands and they leave the meadow and walk toward the river, Adam listening intently as she tells him of her discoveries and of the transformation they can experience. She shares everything and the knowledge causes Adam to feel very important, destined for something greater than this life of Peace, Power, Provision and Protection. Perhaps they can become more than recipients; perhaps they can become facilitators of something even greater.

They sit by the river and eat.

THE EXODUS OF PEACE

I hid in a gully and waited
For passage of time to bring wind of her scent
So near the breath to draw her in
But moment transposed to moment and went
From ocean to ocean and waiting
By copious waves in the night
Yon in the depths a sunken ship's treasure
Moved by the drift but never to light

I rode a train 'cross the villainous prairie
And sat in a cave with the dubious dead
My query echoed in visionless sockets
Look where you lost her their severed tongues said
Once on the breast of a verdant pasture
Once risen from dust and anointed as king
Always the theme of the patriarch's novel
Never the rust on the prince's bright ring

Some say he will speak her to me
But noble she lies in slumber
Wakened and off as a lofty balloon
Counted among the prohibited number
Lost on the wing of a misguided eagle
Melted away on a fallen snowflake
Burned to the ground in the forest's combustion
Washed to the sea when the levees break

They mourn for her at the gates of Eden
They weep for her in the heart of war
They shoot her on the cold veranda
They burn her flag on the marble floor

ROXY

Behind a pale, windowless block building containing who-knows-what, a once green (now gray) Dodge conversion van sits on flat tires like a post-apocalyptic eyesore. The van was manufactured to haul families to Disney World and the beach, with giggling children in its spacious cabin having Goldfish and juice, watching animated movies on the VCR, while Mom and Dad chat in the front seats about adding a room to the house or trading the van for the newest model. They play the radio quietly (the oldies station) and reminisce about high school and college, wondering if the kids will remain true to their alma mater or choose other institutions. The van has their smell and bears the remnants of their family experiences. There are Goldfish crumbs under the seats and gummy bears in the cup holders. Hot Wheels cars hide under the floor mats and a few crayons are lodged in those hard to reach places. Some of the memories were still there when the van was traded and remained when it was stolen and abandoned on English Avenue in the heart of the ghetto. The radio, television and VCR were stripped out and the van became a "first come, first serve" emergency shelter for homeless individuals and a convenient efficiency apartment for prostitutes who needed a place to turn their tricks. In 2007 Roxy moved in and the street dwellers bowed out because Roxy had nowhere else to go. Even hardened and callused hearts had room for a little sympathy. After all, she was a solitary country girl trying to survive the only way she thought possible.

It is a chilly November morning but the air is still because winter hasn't blown in yet, but it is coming. The squalling brakes of a transit bus snatch the van's lone occupant into consciousness, though sleep is always shallow and the city's noises constant, uninvited alarm clocks. They are rude reminders that the earth is still spinning and must be reckoned with one more time. Gray hasn't faded to black since the sun last set; this life is just as gray as it ever was, though black will be welcome when it comes. Hungry dogs scavenge for food along the curbs and fences, leaving their wormy feces and putrid urine like advertisements for disease and filth. The woman in the ugly blue house across the empty lot, where a guy sells watermelons in summer and fire wood in fall and winter, yells through vocal cords burned by toxins of varying origins, that she wishes the fool next door would turn down his music. But he can't hear her because he doesn't want to. It wouldn't matter if he did because he wouldn't turn it down anyway. He revels in early morning, profanity-laced lyrics about having sex when you're thirteen, the demands outlined by "baby mama" (demands he has no intention of meeting), and the *innocent* thrill of toting pockets full of money and deadly weapons, all to a thumping beat that defies the spirit of the morning. When Lionel Richie penned the lyrics to "Easy Like Sunday Morning," he was not thinking of this place or this time.

And that stupid bus still rolls up and stops at this corner with an expulsion of air from the brakes that in the wide world of sounds is sister to nails on a chalkboard and sits for a moment before letting no one out, then moves on to make obnoxious noises on the next corner.

Like most mornings, Roxy's first thought is that she is more tired than when she lay down the night before, a paradox she has lived with for years. Her brain is swimming in fog and for a moment she wonders if she is awake or floating on the remnants of a leftover dream. But her ears pick up the sounds from outside with keen sensitivity and in a moment she is fully awake and the hope of dreams is vanquished. She rolls over on the van floor to relieve the pain in her left hip, a gnawing, aggravating pain that has been her companion since Big Mike pushed her down the steps at the Garden Club. After three weeks or so the bruising finally dissipated, but it still hurts at night and sometimes gives her a stab when she is walking. But what's the big deal? This pain can join the others and they can have a picnic together for all she cares. It's been a year and a half since it happened and there is no money to see a doctor or buy medication, so why worry about it? The couple that found her crying in the stair well called 911 and she was taken to the hospital, but care can be skeletal when one falls in the category of "indigent" and has no insurance or money, so she moves through life with pain as a nagging, annoying companion.

Pain gives people like Roxy something to pay attention to. It lets them know they are still alive and their bodies are fighting for survival. If they feel no pain they begin to wonder what is wrong. At times they hope something *is* wrong.

She feels the urge to urinate but knows it will be a while, so Roxy ignores the feeling and adjusts the thin blanket that covers her. She is struck by the smells inside the van and for a fleeting moment fantasizes about a hot shower with Dove soap and lavender shampoo, but the stench is a companion she has learned to live with as well, and it is particularly pungent this morning. She breathes through her mouth but does so with the disgusting thought that she is sucking in a film of filth. She can almost taste it.

The clean aroma of family life is long gone and the air reeks of old carpet that has been trodden on and sat on and lain on by dirty people and animals for a couple of decades, maybe more. Even though the morning is crisp and cool, there is the hint of mildew and something that tends toward corn chips. And the interminable sweat – the sour remnants of visitors who have come and gone but who left their aromatic calling cards. The young woman coughs and fights back the urge to gag. She threw up the night before and her throat still feels strained and raw. She wages war with nausea most mornings, sometimes a winner and sometimes a loser. She needs a cigarette. A quick search of the van produces what she expects, nothing, so she opens the back door to crawl out. The pain in her hip is not subsiding. It is November and the nights and mornings are crisp and cool. It always hurts worse when the weather changes. She tries to brush out her hair with her fingers, but she doesn't like the dry, frizzy feel of it. Whatever, no date scheduled for this morning anyway.

She walks two blocks before encountering another human being. It is Sunday morning and Atlanta's streets are still slow. He is an older man the color of a UPS truck who sports a tarnished brass cane and a growth on his neck. Ralph, she thinks.

She speaks: "You got a cigarette?"

"Naw".

She walks on, hip throbbing and nausea growing. Walking, she wonders if she is pregnant again. *O God, no. I've gotta pee so bad.* The urge takes her mind away from the horrible thought of dealing with another pregnancy, and just as she starts to duck around the corner of an abandoned house to relieve herself the man with the cane hollers, "Hey, somebody at the corner might give you a smoke. Them church folk feeding pancake 'round by the liquor store."

"I'll check 'em" she says and Ralph nods.

After relieving herself on the ground behind the house, Roxy walks on to the corner of Bankhead and Lowery and sees the church group packing up to leave. Most people from the neighborhood are already gone, just a few old dudes sitting on the guard rails. They are dudes who have less than she does, dudes who will ask for something in return if she bums a cigarette. *What the hell,* she thinks, *I guess I'll just buy a smoke. I gotta have one.* She steps into the Shell station on the southwest corner and asks a middle-eastern attendant, "How much for 'Ports?"

"$5.02 with tax" he replies flatly and heavily accented.

"Not the pack" she says cynically, as if he should know. "The singles."

"A quarter" he replies, still flat, and as if *she* should know.

"Gimme one." Before leaving the store she asks for the bathroom key. He hands it to her but not without a disdainful look and comment. "Gotta spend more than a quarter to use the john. Remember that from now on."

"Whatever" she replies without feeling. She curses him under her breath as she closes and locks the door. She urinates again, more convinced than ever that she is pregnant and filled with dread as the reality of it sets in.

Outside. Inhaling deeply, a toxic reprieve. The menthol flavor instantly sours on her tongue and her teeth feel like they are wrapped in tiny sweaters. Another puff, another blow, life goes on, at least for awhile.

She goes back to the van because there is nowhere else to go. It is home sweet home. A smile forces itself out, albeit with bitterness hanging on the corners of her lips as she thinks of the plaque by her grandmother's front door in rural Ohio: WELCOME FRIENDS. *I should get one of those for the van* she thinks. *My tricks would get a kick out of that.* She doesn't even know who the van belongs to. It was abandoned on this corner long before she came to Atlanta. Early on a guy came by a few times and said she would have to have sex with him or he would put her out of his van, so she had sex with him because she had nowhere else to go. Later she found out it wasn't even his van.

When Roxy was a little girl she dreamed of having her own comfortable home that smelled like country cooking and had a WELCOME FRIENDS plaque by the front door. She loved to help her grandmother make beds and fold towels, especially when the towels were dried on the clothes line and came in crisp and smelling like outdoors. She believed one day she would meet a beautiful man, a man like her grandfather who thought she was valuable enough to work hard for and protect. They would have children, at least two, and she would rise early in the morning to make their breakfast and pack their lunches for school. She would bring them home from dreamy expeditions with her soft voice and tender touch, and carry them to the kitchen where they could come to life to the smell of oatmeal or waffles. She would see them to the bus from the front porch, blowing kisses as they rumbled out of sight.

Roxy dreamed the dreams of little girls. Her dolls were her family and the dollhouse their home. They had picnics and went to soccer games. They attended church on Sundays where they absorbed lessons about Moses in the bulrushes, Samson and Delilah, and Jonah and the great fish. And they sang "Amazing Grace, how sweet the sound, that saved a witch like me." She marveled that Grace could save the witch that wrote the song and wondered what the witch looked like post-salvation.

The questions began around age eight: "Grandma, why does my mama not live with us? Why does she never come to visit? Does she not want to know her own daughter? When is the last time you saw her? Can I see her?"

Roxy knew her mother was alive. She had overheard conversations between her grandparents that made her believe her mother was in Cleveland and that she had personal problems, but they never discussed the specifics of her situation in Roxy's presence. There were a few pictures around the house, all of which were taken when she was a child or teenager, mostly school pictures and photos at family gatherings.

When they were first offered there were no real answers to her questions, but she continued to ask until bits of information started to come. By the time her thirteenth birthday arrived, Roxy had learned that her mother was sent to a home for unwed mothers when she was seventeen. The home was somewhere in northern Ohio (they did not disclose exactly where) but that she had met "friends" in the home who talked her into leaving after the baby was born and "working" for their boss in Cleveland. The baby, of course, was Roxy. The grandparents went for the baby - "Liz" as Grandma called her, "went to the streets and disappeared."

Liz's parents seemed very sad when they spoke of her, and when asked why they did not try to get her to come home simply replied, "We gave up a long time ago."

There was no answer concerning Roxy's father. "We don't know who he is or where he is." She had only asked twice and concluded by her grandmother's tone that she should not ask again.

Teen years brought more questions but Roxy dealt with them in her own mind since there seemed to be little else to extract from her grandparents. She was confused by the idea that any mother could live knowing she has a child and not want to know that child. *Does she not want to see me?* Roxy wondered. *Does she not care what I look like, how I am doing in school, what I like to eat, what my hobbies are? Does she think of me on my birthday?*

Birthdays came and went, as well as Christmases, summer breaks from school, piano recitals, PTO programs, shopping trips for new clothes and all the other things that accompany childhood. They came and went until finally Roxy began to lose interest in them all. She felt a growing void in her heart and began to search for ways to fill it. She migrated to other kids in her school that seemed to identify with her situation, and soon she was smoking marijuana, drinking, and sleeping with any boy that gave her attention.

Roxy became best friends with a girl named Melinda, a cynical child whose father was an obnoxious alcoholic and whose mother allowed him to intimidate and run over her and the kids at will. From the time she was fourteen Melinda vowed she would leave home as soon as she turned seventeen. She had done her homework and learned that seventeen year-olds have a legal right to leave home and go where they want. Melinda looked forward to the day of her freedom, and for some inexplicable reason fantasized that Atlanta was the place where her dreams would come true. She had never been to Atlanta but there was something about the sound of the southern city's name, something compelling about living in the south that made her think everyone there would be friendly and there would be no end to the opportunities she would find. She pictured herself sitting on the upstairs veranda of her neatly decorated townhome, the climate perpetually warm and pleasant, the lights and sounds of Turner Field off in the distance. Melinda's dad loved to drink beer and watch baseball, and the Braves were familiar because of their national television coverage. It seemed the weather was always just right at Braves games, and the people were vintage Americana. Surely they represented all southern folks. Yes, Atlanta or bust.

As Roxy and Melinda grew closer, the dream of escaping the problems that plagued their young lives became a corporate dream and they began to plan their getaway. As the partying increased and the priorities shifted, school became less and less important, so to bail out short of graduation was no big deal. Of course, youthful minds do not usually consider the little things necessary to survive on one's own, such as money for rent, utilities, groceries, transportation and all the incidentals that arise in an ordinary life. Little thought was given to the kinds of careers available to young girls that fall a little short of a high school diploma. The girls believed by some natural order their dreams would evolve into reality without effort and they would share an apartment and do what they wanted for years to come.

Melinda devised a plan for getting to Atlanta. The weekend following her birthday they would get a friend to drive them a few miles to the truck stop near Interstate 75. They would meander around the parking lot and restaurant, spreading the word that they were looking for a ride south. She was sure their pretty faces and big smiles would land them a quick hitch, and she was right. One trucker said he was heading from Cincinnati to Baltimore, but could probably "detour" through Atlanta. He winked at Roxy when he said it, but he was an old-timer with greasy hair and snuff juice on his shirt, so the girls declined and told him they didn't want him to go so far out of his way just for them, but "thanks for the offer."

Chuck was a different sort altogether. He was younger, well-built, thick blonde hair that fell in the back from under a leather cowboy hat. He was nice and told the girls he could have them in Atlanta the next day. He seemed genuine and helpful, not shady like some of the truck stop's patrons. He asked them if they had eaten and paid for pancakes and juice. They thanked him and accepted his offer to ride to Atlanta. He said, "No problem." He removed two small tablets from a pill bottle in his jacket pocket and swallowed them with gulps of black coffee. "These are my helpers" he informed them. "The road gets long and boring and the pills help me stay awake and attentive. It only takes a second for a big rig to get out of control and very bad things can happen." They nodded and were glad he was taking measures to get them safely to their destination.

Chuck's truck was a purple Kenworth and the girls giggled with excitement as they boarded. Their dream was actually coming true – a free ride to the city of their fantasies with a good-looking trucker in a cool, purple tractor. The cab was spacious and comfortable and the dash looked like a spaceship. Behind them was a roomy sleeper with a television and pictures on the walls of race car drivers and women in bikinis.

"Wow" Roxy exclaimed. "You could live in here."

"I do, most of the time" Chuck replied. He guided the long rig down the onramp and onto the Interstate, shifting gears every few seconds as they accelerated. They soon reached seventy miles per hour but had only traveled about twenty miles when Chuck exited at a rest area, telling the girls he needed a "potty break." When he re-entered the truck he immediately asked, "Do you girls like to get high?"

Roxy and Melinda were taken aback by the unexpected question and the straightforward manner in which it was presented. They looked at each other and Melinda shrugged her shoulders. "Yeah, we like to smoke a little weed sometimes. Why, do you have some? A little purp in your purple truck would be fun." They all laughed.

"I have something better than that" Chuck replied, once again straight to the point. He reached into the same pocket the pills came from and produced a snack-sized Ziploc bag with tiny stones in it that looked like broken quartz. "Have you ever had any of this?" he asked. "It's kinda like speed that you smoke. It really gives you a nice buzz but doesn't make you sleepy like pot does sometimes."

"What's it called?" Roxy asked

"Oh, they just call it 'rock' up here. It's actually legal in Ohio" he lied. He pulled out a little glass tube and said, "Here's the pipe if you guys want to try it. It's really no big deal, and if you don't like it at first we can forget about it and smoke some weed."

Crack cocaine. A miniscule pipe, constructed of glass, brass, or whatever is handy. A nondescript stone the size of half the pinky fingernail, crude like jagged, foggy quartz, entirely uneventful in its presentation. Quick application of fire and a deep draw on the pipe, careful to consume the length and breadth of its vapor. The effect is dynamic release of massive amounts of dopamine in the brain, producing, by most accounts, the most explosive alteration of the brain's natural function known to man. The euphoria lasts but a few moments, but from the second of its expiration the brain screams for repetition of the event: Instant addiction.

A seven hour trip from Cincinnati to Atlanta became two days as Chuck stopped at nearly every rest area and truck stop along the way to get the girls high and take advantage of them. Seeing the drug made them shake and stammer and they would do anything to get it. Once, Roxy found herself in the floor board of the truck, scrounging for a piece of the drug no bigger than a pinhead that fell from the pipe. From the sleeper Chuck laughed and called her a stupid b---h. He returned to his evil deeds inside the sleeper.

The girls wondered what he would do when it was all gone, and they soon found out. In the pleasant pre-sunrise of a Monday morning, Chuck steered the rig onto the Bankhead Highway exit off I 285, Atlanta's bypass, and into the parking lot of a truck stop. He told the girls to go to the bathroom while he went for coffee. When they returned, Chuck and his purple truck were gone. They stood for several minutes without speaking, just staring toward the highway as if someone was on the way to rescue them, but no one came and eventually Melinda spoke, "Well, we wanted to come to Atlanta, right? We are here and everything's gonna be fine. I think we should find out where we can get a room. We've got about four hundred dollars so we can afford to stay in a hotel one or two nights, then we need to find an apartment. I bet we can get one for two hundred, and then we'll find jobs." Roxy found little comfort in her friend's words. This place looked, smelled and felt so much different than her expectations, and the physical and emotional remnants of the trip from Ohio lay on her like dirty rags.

Melinda asked a potbellied trucker if he knew where there was a decent hotel, and he pointed back across the Interstate, away from the city; however, their confidence in truckers had been destroyed, so they began to walk east toward the high rise buildings of downtown Atlanta.

They could see the skyline marked with impressive architecture and were a little excited and a lot afraid. The reality of being there held a different emotion from that of their dreams. This new emotion was more ominous and foreboding. They felt overwhelmed.

Worst of all, the young immigrants had no idea what the stretch of asphalt between them and those tall buildings had in store. They were absolutely unaware that their dreams were about to be expunged and their hopes amputated by shadowy figures that dwelt in and around the opaque houses of this neighborhood. Chuck was slick and manipulative but there were parasites on these streets that saw them as more than a few hours of fun. They were now targets for a much more malevolent category of manipulator. They were viewed as tools for making profits, much like a tractor to a farmer or a sewing machine to a seamstress. They walked a mile or so and spotted a Checkers burger stand on the corner ahead.

"You hungry?" Melinda asked.

"I'm starving" Roxy replied. "Wonder if they are open?"

It was a twenty four hour a day establishment, so they ordered two burgers and a Coke to share and sat down at an outdoor table. A young man in baggy jeans, white t-shirt and a Padres baseball cap cocked sideways watched them from the next table, and when they finished, made his approach. "I ain't seen y'all 'roun here before" he declared, his smile revealing gold lining around his top teeth. "What's y'all names?"

"I'm Melinda and this is Roxy. Nice to meet you. We're new in town and actually could use some help finding a place to stay." Melinda extended her hand toward their new friend and he eagerly took it, holding on a little longer than she was comfortable with, but she smiled to cover her anxiety and he smiled back.

"I run a little business out here helping folk with stuff like findin' somewhere to stay, or hookin' 'em up with what they need, you know, jus' making an honest living and taking care of folk, you know what I'm sayin'?" He reached into his pocket, withdrew a small baggie and placed it on the table in front of them. The sight of the bag and the white stones inside brought a visible reaction from both girls. Roxy's mouth opened and popped shut with an involuntary clicking of her teeth. Melinda adjusted the collar on her jacket and began to twist a strand of hair that her fingers encountered.

"Oh, I see you ladies have seen some o' this before" the young man declared. "Hol' on a minute. I'll be right back." He picked up the bag and stepped away from the table. The girls followed the hand containing the bag as its owner walked a few feet from them and put a cell phone to his ear. They could hear the conversation but cared about nothing but the contents of the bag.

"Big Mike" he spoke. "This ya boy, Shawty. Can you come 'round here by my corner, I got some folk you need to meet. Alright, I be here."

Seven Years Later

The afternoon staggers into night and two a.m. is lost somewhere in a black vacuum between Sunday night and Monday morning. Roxy is walking again, walking that same hard, gray path from the corner of MLK to the corner of Simpson, about three-fourths of a mile, but who's counting? Simpson is now Joseph E. Boone Boulevard, but to most folks in this neighborhood it is still just Simpson. Why change what is familiar, even if it is horrible?

She walks, purposeful but aimless, resolute but without concern for destination other than that corner, or a stranger's car, whichever comes first. She walks past men sitting on block walls or leaning against light poles or strolling down the sidewalk like noon on a Thursday in a quaint Ohio town, but rarely does she pass without their attention.

"Hey, baby, what you lookin'?" or "Come on, sexy, you know, you, me, a couple a Colts an' a blunt" or "Hey mama, you lookin' for me? Well, here I am, mmm, mmm."

But she knows them all and she knows they have no money, or Colts, or blunts, so she keeps walking. There's not a turn of the head or curl of the lips or change in the gait, just walking. But a BMW slips along the shadowy boulevard, moving west from the direction of Northside, slow and effortless and quiet like a yacht moving through night enshrouded swamp water. She stops because he probably does have money, the car and all. She doesn't know him, just that he drives a nice car and he is white, probably some poor, unsuspecting, middle-aged white lady's knight in shining armor. The kind of man Roxy has never really known, but countless times has *known*.

The car slows and the passenger side window drops silently. They negotiate as if she is selling nick-nacks at a flea market and she opens the door and slides in. Thirty minutes later he drops her at the same spot and she walks again under the same intrusive gazes from the street's night dwellers, but to a new set of comments because they know where she's been.

She walks back to the van and vomits behind it before getting in. She tucks the two twenty dollar bills deeper into her bra – survival. She lies down and pulls the smelly cover to her chin. She thinks about Ohio and her grandma's little wooden house, how you couldn't stay in the sitting room when the fire was stoked because it was so hot, how the smell of fried pork chops and cornbread would greet her when she got off the school bus, how Grandma called her "Roxy baby." She smiles and a tear drops to the floor of the van.

She lost track of Melinda a couple years back. Big Mike moved Melinda to Cleveland Avenue and a ratty stretch of real estate between Interstates 75 and 85, notorious for drug activity and prostitution. Big Mike went to jail when one of his "girls" was shot in the leg when Mike's van was caught in the crossfire of a battle between low level drug runners. He took her to Grady Hospital where attendants discovered she was fourteen years old. She admitted to prostitution and was in possession of drug paraphernalia. Her "boss" was arrested on the spot for contributing to the delinquency of a minor. As they led him from the emergency room in handcuffs, he vowed that upon his release he would find the girl and "set things right." Melinda stayed in the Cleveland Avenue district, now free to run her own business and keep her own money. She had regular customers and things had become familiar. Why tamper with what is familiar, even if it is horrible?

Roxy is familiar with Simpson, MLK and Bankhead. She, too, is free from the oppressive hand of her overlord, at least for now. She thinks back over her life and remembers the dreams of a little girl. Well, she made it to

Atlanta, although there have been no cozy townhomes with iced tea on the veranda, as Melinda described. The summers are blazing hot and winters "four blanket cold" as her grandma used to say, albeit without Ohio-like snows. She has two children, so far, both born while she was incarcerated. They live in foster homes and may one day ask the same questions she asked as a child: *Where is my mother? Does she not want to see me...?*

And she has never been to a Braves game.

Roxy drifts off to sleep and dreams of a rose garden surrounded by trees of dazzling colors like she's never seen, and the beautiful man of her dreams lies beside her in a bed of rose petals.

SERPENTS AND SANDSTORMS

Shawn sits across from me and fills the room with his electric smile. Sky blue eyes dance lightly, examining pictures of my children and die-cast models of antique cars on shelves chocked full of fatherhood. He offers his opinion on the differences between old cars and new ones. "Mostly crap with a few exceptions" he calls the newer models. "But this" he says with a tone of complete respect, as he eyes a 1973 Dodge Charger, "this is a real car, a man's machine." He blows dust from the top of the shiny red toy and places it back on the shelf. I reminisce a moment about a doctor I remember from my childhood who owned two Plymouth Roadrunners with high trunk spoilers, both adorned with cartoon roadrunner artwork. He was the envy of every real man in the community, except Bobby Payne with the '68 Camaro, a mechanized beast with a 396 and Hurst shifter, which leaves all other car memories in a cloud of southwest Virginia dust. I will never forget the sticker in the back window. It displayed a chubby fist with the middle finger standing at salute. I guess if anything qualifies a man to flip off the world, holding the title to a '68 Camaro does. I always remember the bad things.

"They don't build 'em like that any more" Shawn reflects. He moves to the next shelf and comments on how pretty my girls are, says one day I'll have boys lined up on the driveway, asks slyly if I'm sure I am the father, says with a mischievous grin that one of them "looks like Carl, the mailman." Back to cars: "Do you still have the '66 Galaxie?"

"Yeah, it's in the back of the warehouse and will probably be there when I'm an old man" I reply. "You know how old cars are and how much money it takes to fix one up. It's a '67 by the way."

"Huh?" he grunts.

"The Galaxie's a '67 but they are basically the same car with mainly a little difference in the front end. You see, the grill on a '66 is flat but…" My explanation fades because Shawn has already moved to a picture of my family at Yellowstone National Park and is more interested in the decorative wolves that frame the photo than the touristy clan posing in front of Old Faithful. "Did we look like goobers or what?" I joke.

"Naw man. That's a cool picture. I'd like to go out there sometime. I'd like to see one of them wolves in the wild. Or maybe a moose. Did y'all see any moose?" I start to answer that we had, in fact, seen a female moose from a distance, but Shawn is on a roll and will not hear me anyway, so I nod and continued to listen.

"I hear there's elk everywhere that'll walk right up to your car, walk right down the street in some western towns. Them things are big, man, it's like all the animals out there are bigger. Like the wolves, man. Most people don't know how big a full grown wolf is. They think it's like a dog or something. Naw, man, a grown wolf would come up to here" he declares, leveling his hand across his chest. He rambles on about grizzly bears and debates with himself about size differences between grizzlies and polar bears, concluding that the latter are taller but grizzlies are thicker, therefore heavier. Grizzlies land the top spot, according to Shawn, and having resolved this great zoological debate he sits back in the chair and folds his hands behind his head. Sweat stains have yellowed the armpits of his shirt. A smile starts in the middle of his mouth and emanates to the corners. I know another resolution is coming. "But you won't catch no better fish out there than I can drag in right here." He finishes the declaration and sighs like a man who just polished off a plate of pot roast and gravy-slathered taters, a task he has obviously completed frequently during his life. He has pronounced the gospel of Shawn. The truth has been told, and as far as he is concerned we can call it a day. This man knows his fish and is darn proud of it.

I decide to leave Wyoming with its enormous mammals, albeit unremarkable fish, and broach another subject. "So how are *you*?" I ask. The question changesShawn's mental geography along with mine and I can almost see the big mouth bass swimming in his brain jump and dive into the black depths of Shawn's favorite fishing hole and disappear. The smile runs away and his eyes shift to an empty spot on the wall. They are two blue pools in his wide face and the blue seems to change shades, now the sky in Indian summer, now graying like those of a Husky or Malamute, now dark like pewter.

"I'm doin' alright, man. Since I been here, I mean. You know, I mean, as long as I keep comin' around here, but work and all, you know. I mean, I know what I need to be doin'." He stumbles through the rhetoric, sucking short breaths through tar-stained lungs and wiping sweat beads from his forehead. His eyes scan the pictures on my office walls. He is not comfortable with the change of subjects. He asks if my son is still playing drums and I say he is playing "all the time."

The topic of music brings back some of the sparkle and he says, "I'd like to see him play some time. I always wanted to be in a rock band. I love the jam bands, man. I love to sit and listen to dudes who can just bring it all night long. You know, it's like they just make up songs as they go, and ever'body's on the same page, and nobody ever screws it up, or if they do, ever'body just laughs and keeps playin'. You can't go nowhere to find more peace and feel more like family than a good jam. Man, Widespread is coming to Atlanta and I'd give anything to see them again, but I probably ain't gonna have the money, you know."

"Yeah" I agree. "That's real talent." We talk about the guys we think are most talented, guys who don't need computers or gadgets to get the sound right, guys who were born with "the gift" that giftless dreamers want so badly but have to pay for. I mention The Eagles and their "ring of fire." The band members would sit in a circle and improvise tunes, and each member had to bring the goods or be the object of intense disdain and ridicule. Keeping up with Joe Walsh had to be quite a task.

Shawn grins widely and taps his chest with his fist. "And what about Warren Haynes or Derrick Trucks? Just bein' in the room with them guys, man, it's like you know 'em, man. It's like ever'body knows ever'body and ever'body is just family, man, and nobody's givin' nobody else any crap or askin' for nothin', man. And the dude on the guitar, who has made a zillion records and played in front of kings and presidents and has more money than he can spend, well he's just one of us, man! He's just a dude at the party who's havin' a good time."

I comment that the big fat blunt they pass through the audience may have something to do with all that love and comraderie, and we both laugh.

We shift gears and talk about the building project we just initiated at City of Refuge, and about how all the electrical equipment is out of code and will have to be replaced. Somewhere between lighting and transformers he seems to drift to another place and stays there until I ask, "So, you let Gary move in?"

Shawn's expression turns serious and his body language defensive and he launches into a jumbled explanation of his benevolence toward Gary, an unemployed drifter with HIV and a long list of other problems. I knew the minute they met that somehow they would connect in a way that would land them both in a ditch and someone would have to dig them out. I have kept my shovel handy.

"Yeah, I mean he needed somewhere to go and them people he was with, well, he just couldn't take it over there no more. I just can't leave nobody out on the streets. You know, I mean, we ain't got but one bedroom, and we ain't got no money. You know, that's what me and you been talkin' about, but I just can't let him stay out on the streets. The streets'll eat him up. You know Gary, he ain't exactly tough."

Something about his last comment jolts my memory and I leave the room in favor of a southwest Virginia cow pasture and a tackle football game with my brothers and cousins. That field and its theme of advancing a pigskin to the designated goal, populated by shirtless boys in cutoff dungarees, colliding with each other at full speed, and all without the benefit of helmets or pads, was my first measuring stick for toughness. That field and the barn that stood on the ridge above it, with a hay loft that seemed a hundred feet from the ground, where the same group of boys would dare each other to jump from the loft's double doors to a miniature haystack below. That is where toughness was decided, where one's potential for manhood was inseminated or aborted in a whirlwind of ridicule. And those who proved tough enough went on to jump from bridges and drag race their Pintos and Vegas in the middle of the night and drink cheap beer until they puked. They put on pads and helmets for their high school teams and continued to collide with other guys because it was fun and the measure of their perceived toughness hinged on it. And for some it was in locker rooms and on bus rides to collide with tough guys from other schools that they began to discuss ways and experiment with methods of making themselves tougher, and they landed upon the conclusion that advantages in life and toughness can be achieved by taking shortcuts, that there is a faster road to strength and courage and zeal and toughness than the mere processes of hard work and discipline. So they began to use drugs, speed or a snort of coke to get jacked up for the game, a joint to mellow out afterwards, a hit of acid now and then just to prove they were not afraid of it.

But the road of boyhood eventually leads to one last bus ride to one final destination, and the ball is snapped for the last time. There is one last scramble, a final hit, the struggle to walk away as the toughest guy. Like Jack London's "dominant primordial beast," each boy wants to leave his mark, lead the pack, have his name engraved on the wall, have stories written about him, be the legend. The scoreboard announces the winner. The broadcaster gives the statistics. The winning side cheers and the losers begin to think of who to blame. Many boys walk away from boyhood games with strength and resolve that helps them succeed as men and courage and discipline that is born of experiences on the bottom of the pile as well as the top. Other boys leave the field, but never really leave it. Most who artificially enhance their performances are able to leave the drugs in the company of the game and move on with only interesting stories to tell, but there are a few who carry the curses into adulthood and make them part of family, faith and career.

Shawn brings me back to the office with a huge yawn and stretch. I watch him for a moment before I speak, then begin with a low, non-threatening tone. "You don't have to defend yourself, Shawn. I'm not implicating you for anything" I say. "I know you have a great big heart. It's something I have always admired about you, and you love to help people. But Shawn, don't you think you will be able to help people in a more significant way if you will concentrate on getting yourself better first. I mean, you realize that you are not really in a position to offer help to others right now, don't you? *Don't you?*" He shrugs his big shoulders. I continue. "We need to get *you* straightened out. Man, once that happens there's no telling what kind of impact you will have on others." Before the words fall off my lips he is shooting them down.

"I'm doin' better, man, and I think we can all help each other along the way. I ain't gotta be perfect to help a dude with worse problems than me." He isn't angry, just committed. Bringing conviction to a person with such good intentions suddenly strikes me as one of the most difficult things I've ever attempted. It is a simple thing to point out the errors of sacrificing cats or painting graffiti on tombstones; it is quite another challenge to convince a person he should wait a while to do good deeds. For a moment my fading memory calls up a conversation I once had with an inebriated relative after he had overdrawn his beer balance by about a six pack.

"I ain't never tried to hurt nobody" he proclaimed with genuine seriousness. "I just wanted to do good and keep the wheels between the lines." He mumbled something else that was lost in a slobbery slur, something about not meaning all the terrible things he had said about me and that he loved me with all his heart. I contemplated a question – *Why do addicts and alcoholics so often bear such great compassion toward other hurting people?* Shawn's voice summons me once again, dragging my mind from the land of adult ADD.

"I'm tryin' to help Micah too, man. You know, he just can't beat the stuff and him with that new baby and all. Man, Trisha done told him he better get it straightened out or they ain't gonna survive. You know what I mean? And me and Micah, we're keepin' up with Kevin, the blind dude, 'cause he ain't got nobody." Shawn's sincerity is remarkable. I want to hire him on the spot: Director of Love or Compassion Foreman. I have met a few people in my time who exhibit with immediate evidence the tremendous gift of caring for others. They will do without, or at least with less, in order to bless the last, lost and least. They are drawn to people in crisis and hold the belief that two pair of shoes in their closet is an abomination if the beggar on the corner has none. It is this man, usually trudging through life with one tattered pair of shoes, who always drops a dollar in the panderer's cup, even if the cardboard sign reads, "WHY LIE, I NEED A BEER."

Shawn is this type person. Unfortunately, his needs are as great as those of the people he tries to help, or greater. He spends his time, talent and treasure attempting to drag his friends to the surface of their self-made drowning pools, but does so with a millstone chained to his own neck. He offers sincere counsel to younger guys, warning them of the danger of getting involved with the wrong people and the wrong stuff, all the while purveying a "do as I say, not as I do" message, which most curious youngsters reject altogether. Shawn loves deeply but the quicksand of his own addiction continues to suck him downward. By his own account he awakens in the middle of the night gripped with terror that someone he loves is in trouble. He shows up unannounced at the homes and work places of wives and girlfriends of his buddies, frantically insistent that they stop what they are doing and "intervene."

"You have to do something or he's gonna die! Believe me, I know what I'm talking about. The things he is doing will kill him!"

On various occasions Shawn has described to me in great detail the sufferings of his cohorts, but rarely does he want to discuss his own walk along a very thorny path. Only when he sinks to levels of misery akin to manic depression and is without the ability to function does he open up and acknowledge his need for help; however, after a brief visit to the clinic and implementation of a new combination of medications, the future brightens again. He goes back to work as if he has overcome a bout with the flu.

"It's all good, man. I'm doin' alright."

Sometimes at night, as I lie in bed awaiting the blessing of slumber, those words crisscross my mind like the little ball on a screensaver. If you look at it too long it will make you crazy. You just wish the ball would keep going and find a happy resting place, a productive end. But it only bumps the edge and traverses again, trapped in a world that will not let it go. I think my mind will always have those words, and they will bounce around like an echo in a cave. "It's all good man. I'm doin' alright."

I sit back in my chair and watch as Shawn shifts his weight, rising now and then to study various items on the shelves, tugging at the front of his shirt as if its friction on his belly is driving him crazy. He picks up a bobblehead figurine of Michael Vick and laughs like a little boy. He makes a joke about the NFL star's dog fighting troubles, says it is sad that a guy with so much will sacrifice it for something so stupid. I agree. He places the toy back down and grabs his long ponytail, pulling loose the rubber band that secures it and shakes his head until I can no longer see his face. I wait for him to reorganize the mess, then decide it is time to tell the truth. This time there is firmness in the tone.

"Shawn, I have to be honest with you. *You* can't help Gary, and *you* can't help Micah, and *you* can't help Kevin. But if you will commit yourself to the right thing and get *yourself* better, you will be a tremendous friend to all of them and others as well." I say it as if it is law and he will immediately succumb to its requirements and evolve before my eyes. If not a certainty, it is my greatest hope. Sometimes all one can do is pray, hope and declare something as if it is so. Sometimes a stern declaration is offered only as another approach when all other approaches have failed.

For the first time Shawn looks me straight in the face and behind his eyes I see shadows of deception. It is not a deception born of his own intuition, but one that has been deftly implanted in his mind and spirit and which now grips him like the hangman's noose. For some reason I am reminded of a line from Stephen King's *The Green Mile:* "He kills them with their love." I don't really believe Shawn is killing his friends but am firmly convinced his love and compassion toward his brothers is helping to suck away his own chance for survival. The enemy is using Shawn's spiritual gift to distract him from the reality of his own condition. I realize the gray color to which those magnificent eyes evolve from time to time is the result of the shadows that lighten and darken and shift and traverse from their hiding places in the recesses of his mind and make their way into conscious thought. Now I see a storm in those eyes.

I ask him, "How can you expect to help Micah when the two of you have the same problem? You both use the same stuff. One week you get it from him and he tries to help you get through the effects. The next week he gets it from you and the merry-go-round changes directions. I'm not trying to insult you or to drive a wedge between us, but YOU CANNOT HELP HIM." It comes out louder than I intend and I feel the room's atmosphere take on weight. The color of those beautiful eyes evolves to the darkest shade I have yet seen and his mouth tightens.

He answers, "So what do *you* think I should do?" His tone teeters between sarcasm and accusation.

"Shawn, how long has it been since you used drugs?"

"I'm clean three weeks. I'm doin' good, man. You know, I *gotta* stay clean on this new job."

I fight back the temptation to laugh and throw a little sarcasm of my own and instead ask, "How long have you battled your addiction?"

"Since high school. Eight years. Listen, I know where you're going with this and I can't do no long-term program. I gotta make a living. I got a wife to support. I can't go away for no ten or twelve months. Help me get into an outpatient deal. I'll start goin' to them Celebration meetings, or whatever they're called. I can do what needs to be done after work, in the evenings, but I can't leave this job. It pays fourteen dollars an hour!"

"But doesn't it also put you in the company of the person who writes all the bogus prescriptions for you? And besides, if you get completely well you can make forty an hour. I know what you're capable of." I feel myself pleading.

"Naw man, I'm done with that. Me and Micah talked last night and we're done with that dude. I mean, I don't need to go to prison or nothin'." He puts his hands on the arms of the chair, and in case I didn't hear or didn't believe him, repeats his resolution, "I'm done with that." He completely ignores the last part of my retort, the part about his potential.

"Think about it like this" I say, "one year to save the rest of your life. I know it seems like a long time, but you can do it. It took eight years to get you into this mess. You have to make a commitment to do what it takes to walk out of it. One year to commence the next sixty years of happy, healthy living. We will pay the bill. We will pull together resources from family and friends to meet your monthly obligations. We will make sure Anna is taken care of. Come on, man, you have to do this!"

"I'll think about it" he mumbles, but I know the answer.

I am back in Virginia and the cow pasture is alive with hoots and high-fives, the smell of silage and manure hanging in the air like the morning fog. The game is over: 49-42 in favor of the Cowboys, but later in the day the Steelers will get their chance at revenge. We are making our way to the barn, scratching itches ignored during the game and spitting the pasture's residue from our mouths. A new adventure waits inside the barn's gray plank walls. The walk takes us through an apple orchard, its trees flush with their crimson glory and we pick our afternoon snacks, shining them on dirty pants, throwing the sloppy, ragged cores at each other, subsequent thirty second rotten apple war, scattering like sheep from a coyote at the pasture's edge, not wanting to wear rotten apple slop the rest of the day, and definitely not ready to bathe.

In the barn the challenge is presented. An ornery yearling calf, ready for the stock market, is imprisoned in a gated cubicle, nervously and goofily banging into the wooden barriers, entirely bothered by the ruckus created by an unexpected mob of sweaty miscreants. Only the toughest among us will accept this challenge. Only one will jump from the top rail onto the beast's bony back and hold on for dear life until he is thrown against the wall like a bale of hay. The rest of the boys will find excellent reasons to make their way back toward the house. "Aunt Connie's prob'ly lookin' for us," or "Yeah, it's about supper time," or "I think I forgot to turn off the water hose." Likely excuses.

We were boys and we had no idea the plans God had for us. We rambled through our allotment of days making memories out of temporary struggles and momentary victories, subconsciously cherishing the blessings of family, friendship and daily bread. We cherished these things because they felt right. They were warm and comfortable, clean and fulfilling. There was no point of reference by which to measure our innocence. We had no idea there were serpents gliding through the tall grass of our boyhood gardens, waiting for us to break free from the authority of parents who thought obedience was the benchmark of the childhood experience. The serpents blended into the landscape, camouflaged against the limbs of splendid trees, flattened against the terrain of our football pastures, moving silently through the waters of our favorite swimming holes. They patiently awaited our reconsideration of obedience, silently anticipating our individual encounters with and subsequent contemplations concerning Knowledge and Life.

We sledded down snowy hillsides in winter, gripping the sides of a Buick hood big enough to hold a yard full of school children, reaching speeds that made us grit our teeth and strain our neck muscles, barely missing trees that, if collided with, would have sent us all to White's Cemetery at the end of the dirt road. We warmed our hands over the fire at the top of the hill, sipping hot chocolate and inhaling hickory smoke, pulling potatoes wrapped in foil from the coals and attacking them like jackals on a fresh carcass. We slept on the porch of an old train depot that overlooked New River as it wound through the dark countryside, passing the old shot tower and Valleydale Farm, running parallel to the railroad track for what seemed like endless miles. We trekked the fields - drifters with no destination, compelled to move but without cause, moving for the sake of moving. We camped out in the barn loft and held wrestling matches at midnight – Rick Flair vs. Ricky Steamboat, Junk Yard Dog taking on George "The Animal" Steele. "The Animal" always won because he was a biter and we all hated to be bitten. Once the biting began, submission was not far behind.

One morning we awoke in the loft to find a snake skin on a neighboring hay bale. It was unnerving to know reptiles were molting within arm's reach as we slept, but it didn't stop the adventures. We were oblivious to the fact that reptiles slithering past our sweaty little hay-dusted bodies in the night were harmless next to the serpents sent to measure our purposes and orchestrate plans to destroy them. Serpents coiled themselves around tree branches and watched us sled past. They sat in the fire and mused at our appetites, formulating plans to use them against us. They hid in the high grass, moving just close enough to catch our scents, registering everything about us in their memories for future use. They observed our battles (bb gun fights, playing "chicken" in the creek, the wrestling matches and football games) and were humored at the foreshadowing of it all and by the knowledge that our lives would one day be characterized by conflict, and that some of us would lose. When we were children the serpents could not touch us. They were prevented by a hedge of protection resulting from the prayers of our mothers and grandmothers. In my case, they were terrified of my father who wielded a mighty Sword and spoke words that made the serpents cower, but they waited with a measure of patience human beings cannot understand for time meant nothing. They were the world's first terrorists, sent to steal, kill and destroy. They watched from a distance and formulated masterful plans to cheat us out of our destinies. They waited for us to contemplate things we had heard and to question their validity. They waited for our days of independence. As we grew the serpents moved closer, close enough to brush against our hearts and tarnish our love, close enough to spew poison into our eyes and ears, close enough to whisper lies. Eventually, they told us our opinions were better than God's, that this world's Knowledge was the key to our success, and that we could become self-sufficient.

When I was seventeen I left home for college and for the first time lived independently of the government of my father's home. I was raised in a strict "holiness" environment and knew very little of the ways of the world. I had no idea how many serpents were waiting for me and was ill-prepared to face them. They were skilled at manipulation and were masterfully cunning, and they knew my tendencies, strengths and weaknesses. After all, they had watched me since I first glimpsed the light of day in a little hospital room in Loma, Colorado.

When I first left home I was naïve and vulnerable. This combination made me easy prey, but there was always a nagging sense that things were not right. I never became comfortable with rebellion. I tried to become a regular partier but drinking inevitably made me sick. Smoking was cool but physically torturous, and I was afraid of drugs. I tried to have meaningless relationships with women but they always wanted to marry me, something I had no idea how to deal with. When I told one pitifully sweet young lady that I didn't want to see her any more, she wept and said, "I just want you to know you have my heart." I smugly replied, "I just want you to know you have my sweatshirt and I need to get it back." At the time, I didn't realize just how cruel that was. Forgive me ladies.

At twenty-six years of age I made a decision that would set the course for the rest of my life. I had become quite unsettled and restless and knew I was at an important crossroads and the direction I chose would affect the rest of my life. I decided to extract everything I believed and throw it onto an imaginary table. I began the process of evaluating my belief system, bit by bit and piece by piece. I needed to know why I believed and whether the belief was worth retaining. I discovered the vast majority of the items on the table had been passed on to me by someone else (parents, Sunday School teachers, youth camp workers, evangelists, etc.). I knew I must embark on a quest to discover Truth for myself. I must dig into the Word of God and ask Him, by His Spirit, to give me what He wanted me to know. The process continues today and I have re-embraced most of what I believed as a child, but some things were left on the table. As the saying goes, there are no grandchildren in the Kingdom of God, only first generation heirs. Each person must discover God for himself, not have God passed down like antique furniture.

Don't get me wrong. I have not arrived and the serpents still whisper. Sometimes I listen to them and occasionally believe what they say. Most often they try to convince me that I am smart enough and strong enough to take care of myself and that my plans are sufficient to carry me through life and make me successful. At these moments I become horribly opinionated and judgmental, philosophizing like I am Socrates or Aristotle and believing that I am absolutely right. At the end of such days my attitudes and words have been meaningless at best and destructive at worst. The Father wants me to consider His words and His ways and to live in absolute obedience to them.

I know a seventy year-old man who grew up much the same as me. His name is Billy. Holiness was the order of the day and church was as much a part of Billy's life as eating or going to the bathroom. He was taught the Ten Commandments and the Lord's Prayer and can quote the twenty-third Psalm to this day. As a young man serpents began to whisper in his ear, telling him the ministries of the church were invalidated by the hypocrisy of its leaders. He listened and began to lose faith. A trusted relative boisterously proclaimed the Gospel but was revealed as a drunkard and adulterer. Little by little Billy's faith was splintered, and when tragedy struck his foundation was too shaky to hold. His younger brother was struck by a train and killed and a close friend of the family died of cancer at twenty-seven. How can a loving God allow these things to happen? Why would you trust a God who doesn't answer your prayers? Wouldn't you be better off to do your own thing than to serve a God who disappoints and lets you down? I thought they told you God cares for you. If so, why is he making you suffer? Why is he making people you love suffer and allowing them to die? The whispering was incessant.

The questions came like a sandstorm and the man lost his direction. His eyes and ears were polluted by the serpent's venom and the confusion and pain led to depression, alcoholism and rage. He began to take out his frustrations on his family, especially his wife. In fits of uncontrolled fury Billy beat and threatened to murder her. There were times when he stood with a loaded pistol pointed at her face, vowing they were about to "go to hell together," while their daughter stood between them begging him, "Please, please, please don't kill my momma."

After years of torment the wife, Faye, escaped the prison that was once her home, leaving on a Friday night with three children in tow. They made a new life, putting faith in God and believing He could make flowers bloom in a graveyard. She worked hard as a single mother to support her children. Though their lives were difficult, and there were periods of great economic, physical and spiritual struggle, Faye eventually experienced restoration and healing and became a true disciple of Jesus Christ. She embraced the church, even with its flaws, and found fellowship, worship and discipleship to be invaluable. Faye became involved in ministry and presented her daughters and son the opportunity to know the Lord for themselves. Today all three are believers and none have repeated the precedent set by their father. Ironically, Faye leads a support group at her church that reaches out to people who are facing issues related to drugs, alcohol, grief, abuse, domestic violence, etc. The son, a Pastor in North Dakota, is a loving husband and father, raising his sons in the ways of the Kingdom. The middle daughter lived through every parent's nightmare, having a child diagnosed with incurable cancer, but retained her faith rather than giving bitterness its foothold. By the way, the child survived! The oldest daughter, well, she is my wife and the magnificent mother of our seven children.

Billy, on the other hand, fertilized and watered the roots of resentment and bitterness and allowed whispering serpents to move in. Thirty-two years after losing his family, he still describes offenses from the past that he can "never forgive." He wanders alone through life with a sandstorm of lies swirling at all times through his head. Billy is talented, witty and humorous. He tells a story of going to the VA Hospital once to "dry out." While there he received the call from my wife that she had gotten married. The announcement so infuriated him that he snatched the phone receiver from the wall and stormed down the hallway to the bathroom. He violently kicked a stall door inward, unaware that a man was sitting on the toilet inside. The door struck the man on top of the head (I guess he was leaning forward), and he fell to the floor, unconscious. Billy was sure he had killed the poor man, so he headed back to the card table in the commons area as if nothing had happened. Shortly thereafter the stall occupant came staggering back into the room, rubbing his head and blinking his eyes. When asked what was wrong, he replied, "I'm not sure, but I think I got struck in the head by lightning."

When he is sober and clear-minded I can sit and talk with my father-in-law for hours. Because of him I have salmon stew in my life. As a general rule I do not like chicken thighs, but his barbecued leg and thigh quarters will cause your tongue to beat your brains out trying to get to it. That phrase is another gift from Billy. He has loaned me numerous stories that I use to entertain my social circle. I know you want to hear another one.

Once Billy was driving under the influence and ran his pick-up into a ditch (that's not the funny part). He did not want to call the police, for obvious reasons, and did not want to pay for a tow truck, so he walked to the store and called his sister's husband, Ray, to help. Shortly thereafter, Ray arrived and they chained his truck to Billy's. They both got into the cab of Ray's truck, which makes me wonder if Ray had been drinking as well, and attempted to pull the ditched vehicle back onto the road. Instead, Ray's truck began to slip sideways and ended up in the ditch with Billy's, tipping onto its side and sending three-hundred pound Ray sliding down the seat to rest on top of Billy. His rear end plastered Billy's head to the window, cutting off his air supply and causing his life to flash before his eyes. When asked what was going through his mind, Billy says, "All I could think of is how I've been shot at, run over by a car, stabbed, pistol whipped, beaten with a pipe and left for dead, and I survived it all. Now I am going to die with my head up Ray's hind-end!" His only recourse for survival was to bite down on Ray's gluteus, which motivated Ray to hoist himself up and relieve the pressure.

Yes, Billy number one is great company and a fantastic country cook. He was once a talented tradesman and hard worker. As I said, he tells a great story. But the other Billy is angry and dangerous. I have sat under a shade tree in his yard, bathed to my elbows in homemade barbecue sauce, enjoying a glass of sweet tea and a good laugh, and witnessed the exodus of the first Billy and introduction of the second. That's when it is time to load up the kids and go home. I have watched his blue eyes become dark and melancholy, like the sky before a storm, the same passing of shadows I saw in Shawn's eyes. When the second Billy shows up, it is only a matter of minutes before he declares, "I need to run to the store." We all know what that means and we tell him we have enjoyed the visit but we must be going. In a few hours, he will be drunk, belligerent, self-piteous and threatening. The serpents sit on his shoulders and gloat.

Shawn, Billy and I were boys once, but boys become men and have before them the eternal issue of what to do about childish things. This is the thought I have as I sit across from Shawn and I am struck by the irony of what I see and feel. Physically, he is a grown man and has proven he can learn and has the ability to effectuate his learning. He exudes a clever wisdom that acknowledges his years and experience. He inherited qualities from his father that are immediately evident to anyone who knows the elder, a fine man who loves God and raised his sons to do the same. Shawn is knit together with good thread and formed from sturdy cloth, but the paradox of his present confusion and misguided discernment leaves me feeling like I just read a novel that is missing the last chapter. His peremptory responses to my pleading are frustrating and I sense my sympathy is evolving into a callous indifference, a process I loathe because of its seeming contradiction to grace. I want to retain a soft heart and willing spirit toward him and become angry at myself that I cannot. I love him dearly but cannot help him. I am very angry about that.

Shawn hugs my neck and leaves the office, cramming a huge dip of snuff between his cheek and gum as he ambles toward the outside door. He calls me later and asks for "a little help with some gas and groceries 'til payday." I drive to a BP station near Turner Field and pay to fill up his truck with gas. To insure they have food in the apartment I hand him a fifty dollar Kroger card. He shakes my hand and thanks me and says he understands I am only trying to help him, and that he hopes I am not angry that he cannot comply. I say that I'm fine. Shortly thereafter, I hear he has moved to another state and started yet another job.

Two years later, on a winter morning, I am standing under a live oak tree in my yard when a phone call comes from my brother, Bruce. As he speaks, I begin to contemplate a tree from a different time and place, the one God was talking about when He promised death would be the trade-off for disobedience, the tree that led me to this moment. And I begin to learn things I wish I did not know. I ride waves of sentiment I will have to navigate the rest of my life, like a surfer skimming across shark-infested waters, knowing the sharks have the means to devour but understanding as well that staying above them is key to everything. There are things I will never forget and they drum up emotions I should never have known, feelings of sadness, regret, emptiness, anger and fear. Shawn is dead and the serpents smile.

Hot tears chase each other down my face and drop onto brittle oak leaves as I learn the details, as I come to *know* the horrible evidence of a young life lost. A young wife left with one child and another growing in her womb. A dozen "what ifs." A mother's impassioned meltdown. On and on for the next few weeks I am afforded knowledge that twists my stomach and leaves holes in my heart. It is knowledge that feels unnatural and foreign. It relates to situations that seem to mock the idea that we are children of a loving Father. Parents are not supposed to bury their offspring. Grandsons are not supposed to live one-third the life span of their grandfathers. Little boys are not supposed to grow up without their daddys, and young wives without their lovers and soul-mates.

In the whirlwind of thought and emotion, these words rise to the top – *I don't want to know this. I don't want to hear it and I don't want to know it.*

THE TREE OF KNOWLEDGE

O the euphoria of not knowing, the ecstasy of being unaware. A child is stricken with horrors and dies in a Calcutta gutter but my heart beats lightly and my laughter remains because I do not know. In Managua, in the half light of evening, spread out in the full shame of ugly nakedness, lying on a graying mattress propped on sandstone blocks, a cloud of dust in the air from the comings and goings of anxious children, grandchildren and the curious, an ancient and frail matriarch heaves and gasps for breath through diseased lungs, finally conceding to ten decades of struggle, and settles like a heap of pale gray powder onto the bed. Fifteen hundred miles away I stand and cheer as my little boy beats out a slow roller to shortstop and the 7-8 Cardinals take the lead.

There is great contentment in not knowing, profound satisfaction in pure ignorance. We gobble up the evening news, licking our proverbial chops for the tasty center cuts of murder, molestation and mayhem. We cringe and express our disgust, pronouncing our own verdicts and sentences, leveling our disdain, even hatred for evil, all the while wanting to know more, hungry for details. We feast on the fruit of the Tree of Knowledge, excited about the chances and possibilities it affords, challenged to digest its poison provision, anxious to align our destinies with its bounty. What would it be like to if I had no awareness that someone in the world is being raped or murdered at this very moment? What if there was no idea in my mind concerning robbery, molestation, terrorist bombings or war? What if I had never heard of these things?

Since the beginning man has been invigorated by the idea of knowing more than he is created to know. Eve and Adam were tempted by the thought of knowing everything their Father knew. They were guilty of putting themselves on level ground with their Creator. They became convinced that more knowledge would further empower them and provide a greater level of benefit than they already had. The Father's intention was to protect them from things they did not need to know. He knew the children He created would not be able to manage the contrasts between good and evil because they were not God! The serpent convinced them otherwise and Eve and Adam set as precedent for their posterity the idea that man can be equal to God and can achieve the highest levels of human success and gratification on his own.

The Father is not opposed to the pursuit of knowledge by his children, as long as the knowledge they pursue aligns with His purpose for them. In the Garden there were two trees which had special significance – the Tree of Life and the Tree of Knowledge of Good and Evil. The Father wanted His sons and daughters to pursue Life and to discover all the Life He chose for them had to offer. His desire was that they embrace the fullness of His nature and enjoy all the benefits that came with it. Eve and Adam needed only to remain close to the Father and pursue the abundant Life He provided and the knowledge of all that was contained inside His purpose for them. Yahweh's purpose was Life - full, rich, healthy, abundant Life. But man was tempted with knowledge that fell outside the boundaries of the Father's purpose. He desired that knowledge for he wished to be like God. By his act of disobedience, man exalted himself above his Creator and set himself up for catastrophe.

Once I asked the Lord to show me a picture of the enemy. You may call him satan, the devil, adversary or whatever you'd like. I had outgrown the idea that he was a red, diabolical figure with pointed ears, a tail and pitchfork, but still had an image in my mind of an Anton Lavey-ish character standing in the doorway of *Hotel California* with a steely dagger in his hand, while demons back-masked *Stairway to Heaven* in the background. The answer to my request came in the form of a spiritual lesson that evolved in my thinking over a period of weeks.

Lucifer was expelled from Heaven because he desired to elevate himself above God. He chose to worship himself and his own ideas above his Creator. Eve and Adam were expelled from the Garden because they valued outside voices over the Father's voice and elevated their own opinions over His Truth. Their worship was misdirected as well.

The place to which I was directed to meet the enemy was a mirror, for the essence of satanism is ME. The reality of an entity that roams the earth stealing, killing and destroying notwithstanding, it is when he tricks me into believing I can take care of myself that I begin to live in rebellion to the Father and His purpose for my life. It is when the tempter deceives me into believing I should pursue knowledge outside the Father's plan that I begin to lose closeness and intimacy in my relationship with God. Sadly, the more of the world's knowledge I pursue, the less frequently the Father shows up in the cool of the evening to walk and talk with me. I am declaring by my actions that I do not need Him as much as I once did.

It is when the enemy convinces me that my opinions and ideas are good enough to bring me success and satisfaction that I become my own god. In that regard, I become like the devil. The first commandment is: "You shall have no other gods before Me" (Exodus 20:3). In other words, self-dependence amounts to idolatry.

In his quest for fulfillment, man pursues education and information and places the highest levels of human value on both. While there is nothing wrong with higher education, and while information is beneficial in the world in which we live, we must understand that neither will bring the desired result. Only obedience to the Father's commands will do so. If the result of disobedience was chaos, war and death, it stands to reason that the path leading back to order, Peace and life is one of obedience. Man was tempted with 'knowledge and self-reliance, and he put more trust in the voice of the tempter, and in his own ability, than in the Father's instruction.

There is no way to turn back time and undo the decisions of Eve and Adam, but there is certainly a way to live in a spiritual existence that aligns with life in Eden. There is a way to live in an abundance of Peace. There is a way to harbor the Power of the Creator within our spirits, thus living victoriously on a daily basis. There is a way to enjoy perfect Provision as we take the little we have and bless, break and give it away. There is a way to dwell under the canopy of his divine Protection, fully confident and unafraid.

Here is the way: HEAR HIS WORDS AND OBEY.

When Eve and Adam listened to false voices and trusted their own judgments they were expelled from the Garden and pushed out into distant lands away from Yahweh's original purpose. It was as if He challenged them to find Garden life outside His plan. For the first time they encountered pain. They were pricked by thorns, bruised by stones and underwent the excruciating agony of childbirth. They were introduced to war and grief when one of their own children plotted against, ambushed and killed the other. For the first time they felt the effects of sickness and poverty. For the first time they knew what it was like to call out to their Father and receive no reply.

This is the knowledge Eve and Adam bargained for, knowledge that poses the harshest imaginable contradiction to the Father's original intention for His children. It is an education of mortality we have desired; it is the pursuit of understanding and wisdom reserved for the highest levels of deity. But we want it, so we have it.

"But of the Tree of Knowledge of Good and Evil you shall not eat; for if you eat of it you will surely die" (Genesis 2:17).

Long Obedience

This morning I stood under a waterfall and thought about Adam. The frigid water came off the rocks and spilled in glorious succession into a knee-deep pool. I stepped under the torrent and for a moment the pounding of the cold, wet gauntlet on my body took my breath. But I remained and soon breathed easy as the tumbling waters moved from torturous to tolerable to an exquisite massage that no masseuse could equal. I could sense my heart beating with potency, and thought I could feel the blood pumping life to every extremity. My mind was fully alive, firing on all cylinders. I was "high."

I leaned back against a rock, smoothed by the flow for centuries, and observed the sea through the wall of water. I observed the world through Adam's eyes. The waves broke on the reef and the sun's rays glistened on the water's surface. A woman and her child walked past on the white sand, and through the waterfall they were perfect in every way. *I want to do this every morning* I thought. *I want to live like Adam.*

In every part of the world are poetic places that stand as reminders of the Father's original intention for His children. There are places where the light still dazzles, mountains reflect His majesty and seas present their mysteries. But there is no place on earth, no matter how remote or uninhabited, that is more than a few hours away from a metropolis via one form of modern transportation or another. In the city the poetry turns to a jumbled rant with very little rhyme or reason. In Genesis 1, God took a creation that was formless and void and gave it order, light and beauty. He fashioned mankind to live in perfect harmony with the rest of natural creation, but God's order was fractured by man's disobedience and his subsequent education in the ways of good and evil.

I have stood in the wild countryside of Montana and watched in wonder as mountain streams plummeted through the pristine wilderness and dumped into some of the world's most striking rivers. I have stood knee-deep in those rivers and watched spectacular rainbow and brown trout glide by in the clear water. I have heard the whisper of God and felt the brush of His Spirit, the same Spirit that hovered over the chaos as the Father commanded, "Let there be light…" (Genesis 1:3). He still hovers over the magnificence of creation, whether in the untamed and untouched serenity of Montana, or in the heart of the world's cities, where its purity has been covered by the debris of the human experience.

I have gazed out over the Caribbean Sea from a cliff on the south coast of Jamaica and absorbed sights and sounds that could have only proceeded from providence. The combination of sounds is orchestral, and each instrument is meticulously tuned and played to perfection. There are no harsh interruptions, missed cues or keys or omissions. The waves crash against the rocks below in successive ovations to the One who hovers. The warm wind purrs and hums and causes tall grass on the hillside behind me to bow and whisper its acknowledgement to the same Spirit that hovered in the beginning, when the Father separated these waters from this fabulous land. Yes, He still hovers, whether over the raw sanctity of the south coast of Jamaica or in places where the roar of vehicles and planes, honking horns, the intonations of corrupted orchestras or the screams of desperate people drown out His music.

One needs only to view natural creation to begin to understand the contrast between God's original intention for his children and the condition of the world today. One needs only to evaluate the differences between the Garden and the ghetto to reconcile how far mankind has moved away from the original plan. One needs only to walk a few blocks on the wrong side of town to learn that Peace is buried under the rubble of decades of poor choices and disobedience. The Peace of the Garden was sucked away with one bite of fruit and man has been searching for it since. The natural order God created was thrown out of balance and nature began to rebel against man. The earth began its interminable groaning and suffering, longing for restoration of the perfect relationship Yahweh intended with mankind. Hurricanes, earthquakes, tornados, floods, fires, tidal waves, volcanic eruptions and every other form of natural disaster became part of the history of the world. As man continued his pattern of self-worship and self-dependence, disease, torment, chaos and pain flooded the world. Rather than humbling himself in repentance and submission to the Father, man continues to chase tranquility and reprieve, but does so without returning to the lifestyle of obedience required by the Father. We seek out beautiful destinations to visit, "vacations" from the world *we* have formed.

We are fascinated by the stunning beauty of majestic mountains, pristine lakes and rivers, and lush gardens, all because there is an inner spiritual connection between us and natural creation. Life in such magnificent places was originally intended by the Father, and still is.

Although most of us live without conscious thought that what drives us is the desire to return to Garden life, it is this inescapable connection that compels us to seek tranquility. We want Peace on earth. The desire is built into the human spirit and drives so much of our thinking and motivation. Of all that was lost when man yielded to temptation and began to trust his own ideas, the most valuable commodity was Peace, for its forfeiture led to every destructive, self-serving invention of man. In his attempts to rediscover the vanished gift of Peace, man runs to and fro, often using the natural elements of God's creation in his pursuit. He takes the fruit of the vine, created in perfection and intended for the pleasure and sustenance of God's children, and pollutes it and perverts it until it is foul and rancid, then drinks it in pursuit of God's original intention – Peace. Man takes plants and flowers from the field, created in perfection and intended for the ethereal satisfaction and physical provision of God's children, and converts them to be smoked, sniffed or ingested, all in attempt to replace what was lost – Peace. Man takes woman, that beautiful blessing formed from his own flesh and bone, sent to resolve his loneliness and provide to him someone with whom Garden life could be shared, and uses her to promote himself and satisfy his lusts, all in attempt to feel as good about himself as the Father originally intended. Sadly, many women listen to the voices of deceivers, as Eve did. They are weak-willed, and in their own quests for the Garden's sensual satisfactions are blown about by deceptive winds. Our motivations toward acquisition of Peace and satisfaction are initiated by the subconscious desire to have the Garden life in the presence of our Heavenly Father that is rightfully ours; however, our methods are usually misguided.

Recently, I have realized more vividly the tragedy of the human condition as it relates to Father's original plan. The literal and symbolic contrasts of my own life are striking. For example, I live in the country on a wooded tract of land, but I work in the concrete jungle. At night I can stand in my yard and see the brilliance of space above me with its fascinating constellations and mysterious planets. I can hear hoot owls, tree frogs, whippoorwills and an occasional bobcat. In the city the stars are hard to see because of the lights and smog, and the sounds are not as pleasant to the ear. Shouting, screeching tires, sirens and an occasional gunshot are harsh contrasts to country life. My house is hidden in the woods, a thousand feet off a country road and out of view of other houses and people. I can change clothes on the back porch without fear of being seen. Much to my wife's dismay, our boys view every tree as a potential urinal. It seems little consolation to her when I say, "It's alright, honey. That's the way I grew up." Her response is usually something like, "That explains a lot of things."

In the city I sometimes see a person without all the garments needed to hide his private parts, and it is not uncommon to witness a guy urinating behind a dumpster or against the wall of a building, but the atmosphere is different. There is more of a harshness or vulgarity to it. In our part of the city, most things seem dirty or tainted. The colors are drab and dull, the buildings and houses often shabby and unkempt, much more trash than in the country. And there is something about burglar bars that adds abrasiveness to the environment. At home we still sometimes forget to lock the doors.

When I was a kid the river and the railroad track were fascinating elements that produced wonder and aroused a sense of adventure. The rivers of southwest Virginia were like wise old men, full of history and quiet passion, and they would share it if someone would sit and listen. Though chronologically ancient, the rivers were full of life and inspiration. The valleys around them were rich and fertile and the fish pulled from their drinks were legendary. The railroad tracks wound majestically through the Virginia countryside and were so indelibly attached to the landscape it seemed they had been there since the world was formed. I walked the tracks with my brothers and friends, anesthetized by the Peace that surrounded them and challenged to know about the world toward which the engines and boxcars chugged.

Ironically, there are rivers and railroad tracks in the inner-city of Atlanta as well, but they present themselves much differently than those of my youth. I have discovered where the trains that rumble through America's sleepy towns and serene countryside go. They come to Atlanta and run right behind the City of Refuge warehouse, and along the way they are etched with gang-related graffiti and vulgar messages for people who sit at the crossings to read. At night burglars take advantage of the noise of passing trains to smash window glass and enter buildings and cars

71

to steal things. The railroad track that crosses Joseph Boone Boulevard is no peaceful implement where boys place pennies to be flattened by passing trains into little copper flapjacks. Rather, it is an easy escape route for thieves who break into our buildings. Don't leave money on these tracks, not if you want it back.

The creeks and rivers that pass through the city are perpetually dark and dirty. The fish that inhabit their waters are not fit to eat, sad victims of pollution most of us don't want to hear about. The Chattahoochee, Atlanta's best known river, garnished most of its fame as the dumping ground for the corpses of children murdered by a serial killer in the early '80s. The banks of the Chattahoochee and other urban waterways are lined with debris, such as plastic bags hanging from fallen limbs, candy wrappers and chip bags (remnants of some of the ghetto's most popular food staples), household garbage, old tires, rubbish from past floods, etc. Neither the Chattahoochee nor its tributaries are monuments to the creative prowess of Almighty God; rather, they serve as sad symbols of the deprecation of all creation.

Though usually buried under the rubbish piles of our own thinking, there is within each of us the knowledge that we were created to live in perfect harmony with God and His natural creation. We were made to live in the Garden and to walk with our Father in the cool of the evening. We were made to love and respect each other and to bless and fulfill each other's lives. We were made to reflect the image of the Creator and to honor Him in all things. However, often this knowledge is unattainable on our own. Our lives have produced such enormous heaps of garbage that we cannot possibly see with clear spiritual vision and hear with open spiritual ears. We need help.

Perfect Peace and Provision are still the Father's intention for His children. He continually offers us chances to experience bits of His Peace, but His true desire is that we begin to walk the path of obedience that leads back to the Garden, where Peace is constant and tranquility a way of life. The earth groans and cries out, anxiously awaiting the return of the true sons and daughters of Yahweh. As long as man continues to trust his own ideas and to rely on his own intellect, we can only expect to catch glimpses, but never to live in the fullness of the Father's Peace. Just out of sight of the glorious day we are having, with brilliant sunshine, cool breezes and puffy clouds is the next hurricane or tornado that will ravage the earth and turn lives upside down. Just beyond that stately, snow-capped mountain is a wildfire that will burn the beauty black and terrorize everything and everyone in its path. Just out of sight of tropical paradise is a fault line that will eventually shift, rocking the ground and the lives of unsuspecting souls, sending waves to wash over our temporary tranquility.

In his quest for spiritual satisfaction, man busies himself with all sorts of carnal pursuits, thinking one day he will happen upon the answer. In 2008, nearly 486,000 new patents were applied for in the United States alone. Patents represent only a small percentage of actual inventions, and the U.S. is only one nation in a world of unsettled people. Man is searching for something to make life easier, thriftier, more fulfilling.

Each year billions of dollars are spent on medical research as experts attempt to find cures for debilitating and deadly diseases. Man realizes he is not meant to suffer, so he looks for ways to minimize his physical maladies and extend his life. There is a subconscious understanding in each of us that our bodies should be beautiful and fully functional, so we spend billions on health foods, fitness club memberships and exercise equipment. We are supposed to feel good and look good, and we expend great energy and lots of money trying to make it happen.

When Sally looks in the mirror, she does not see what she wants to see, so she schedules an appointment with a plastic surgeon. When Mary looks in the mirror, she sees more than she wants to see, so she commits to the next new diet fad, or calls for consultation about liposuction. When Carl looks in the mirror, he realizes he was much more handsome with hair, so he begins to save money for hair replacement. Whether it is tanning, dyeing, or decorating ourselves with tattoos, human being continually strive to remain young and attractive.

While the things mentioned above may not be evil or worthy of judgment, one should not ignore the root cause of man's dissatisfaction with himself. Man was created to be beautiful and healthy. He was created in the image of his Father, and God is not ugly, sick, deformed, overweight, underweight, out of shape, or in any other way unappealing. Man's disobedience continues to result in many forms of hardship, including physical enigmas. While his efforts may provide temporary improvement and relief, man alone will never discover the permanent outcome he is searching for. We can only continue to lament with Mick Jagger, "I can't get no satisfaction."

The Father's plan is still the same as it was when he lifted His highest creation from the dust of the ground and sat him down in a place called Eden. God's purpose for humanity has not changed. Likewise, the method by which we can realize fulfillment of His plan and purpose is as it has always been: Obey Father's words. It was all He asked of Adam and Eve, and it is all He asks of us.

"If you listen carefully to the voice of the LORD your God and do what is right in His eyes, if you pay attention to His commands and keep all His decrees, I will not bring on you any of the diseases I brought on the Egyptians, For I am the LORD who heals you" (Exodus 15:26).

The Lord says OBEY! If you want the Promised Land, OBEY! If you want the Peace of the Garden, OBEY! If you want to be delivered from the bondages of addiction, depression, poverty, bitterness, anger, fear, sickness, OBEY! If you want to enjoy good health and be satisfied with yourself, OBEY! If you want to float like a hot air balloon above this world's troubles, OBEY!

In the passage above, the children of Israel had been delivered from slavery in Egypt because of the obedience of Moses to the instruction of the Lord. They had witnessed, and been part of, one of the greatest miracles ever recorded when the Red Sea parted and they walked through on dry ground. They had watched the army of their enemy perish in that same sea. They traveled three days and needed water. They came to a place called Marah and found water, but it was bitter and undrinkable. The same beneficiaries of the aforementioned miracles complained against their leader and demanded to know what they were to do about water.

Oddly enough, Moses did not form a committee to discuss resolutions to the water shortage problem. He did not implore assistance from the intellectuals or scientists in the crowd to invent a method of making bitter water sweet. He did not send out scouts to determine if sweet water was nearby. In other words, Moses decided against the human approach to crisis and trouble; rather, he immediately called out to his Father and asked for instruction. The Father designated a certain tree that was to be cut down and thrown into the water, another simple command that likely seemed foolish to the general population. But Moses had established a pattern of consulting with his Father and responding in obedience to what he heard, and he had witnessed the results. Trust was a way of life, for he had been faithful in Egypt and had witnessed the calamity resulting from Pharoah's disobedience. Every time Moses had obeyed a command from Yahweh, the promised result was delivered. Moses threw the tree into the waters at Marah and they instantly became sweet (see Exodus 15).

In yet another powerful promise to His children, the Father followed up this tremendous miracle by assuring them that obedience will *always* result in blessing. "Heed the voice of the Lord your God…" and the locusts and frogs that torment you will disappear. "Give ear to His commandments…" and the pure water of life will always be available. "Keep all His statutes…" and natural creation will be your friend, not your enemy. "Do what is right in His sight…" and the Light of His revelation will continually dispel the world's darkness. Hear and obey, and you will not experience the diseases "brought on the Egyptians." He is the "Lord who heals…" and His promise of healing is real but is ALWAYS contingent on our obedience.

The Word of the Spirit is always going forth. It is not dependent on my ability or willingness to see, hear or understand. It is going forth, regardless. It is my responsibility to put myself in position to see, hear and understand. I must reject wrong voices and order my life to minimize stress and fatigue and refuse to allow the garbage truck of carnal living to dump its loads into my heart and mind. I must align myself to receive His words and pictures, and I must respond to what I receive in obedience, and my obedience must be complete.

Whoever has ears to hear… can hear.

Whoever has eyes to see… can see.

Whoever has a mind in alignment with the mind of the Spirit… can understand.

Whoever has a pure heart… can house the words and pictures of God.

What is the key to open ears, clear vision and an acceptable heart and mind? Obedience! Obedience is everything! Simple obedience to what is right will remove callus from the eyes, unclog ears and flush out hearts and minds so the Word of the Spirit may become life. But it must be an obedience that is characterized by perseverance and steadfastness. It must be enacted minute by minute, hour by hour, until the days and weeks turn into months and years.

German philosopher Friedrich Nietzsche said, "The essential thing in heaven and earth is… that there should be long obedience in the same direction; there thereby results, and has always resulted in the long run, something which has made life worth living." The Father's instruction to Eve and Adam in the Garden was simple: Pursue Life and reject the temptation to balance good and evil. Do what is right and leave alone that which falls outside the Father's purpose for you. Exercise a long obedience in the same direction, His direction. Morning by morning rise and remain obedient to His Words. Therein lies the abundance of His Peace, Power, Provision and Protection. Any other path leads only to destruction.

Too often we call out to God, but with reservation, and the Spirit's wind filters and evaporates the prayer before it reaches the Father's ear. He does not receive petition that is laced with the poison of selfishness. He does not hear supplication that has ME as its central theme. He does not expend divine energy on requests that lack total abandonment, that reserve anything, no matter how small or seemingly insignificant. Jesus said, "Unless you forsake *all*…." For many of us it may only be one small thing that keeps us in desert places outside the Garden's gates. We desire, even expect to be rewarded with Peace, Power, Provision and Protection because we sacrifice *something*, even *almost* everything. Compromise is our business. It is our game, except when it comes to the idea of reward. We want the full reward, but we want to reserve something of obedience.

But the Father understands I can't be perfect. No one is perfect. We all have our weaknesses. His grace is sufficient to cover my weaknesses. His forgiveness is available for all my sins, past, present and future.

Father, I want you to hear ALL of my prayer. I want, no, I EXPECT (I claim it in Jesus' name) you to give to me without reservation – to meet ALL my needs according to your riches in glory. I don't want you to hold anything back. I want ALL of you.

But, please understand, I can't give ALL of me. There is that "one little thing." I know you understand. You created me and you know I love you. I respect you and fear you, but I can't give you that "one little thing."

Remember Shawn's words: "I gotta make a living. I got a wife to support. I can't go away for no ten or twelve months."

The wind of revelation is blowing away the fog. I pray it will vanquish the pretense and reveal TRUTH in its complete, unpolluted form. It is that "one little thing" that resulted in eviction from Eden. There was only one rule, one mandate and one condition. By the ONE instruction the Father was asking His children to trust Him when it comes to issues of good and evil. He commanded them to reject the desire for any knowledge of spiritual contrasts, leaving those issues to their Creator. He knew that the "knowledge of good and evil" would present to mankind more than he could assimilate into his mind and emotion and that man could only be reactionary in his responses to that knowledge. He knew that man would begin to trust his own judgment and formulate his own ideas. The Father knew man would begin to seek for pathways to restoration, and that conversation, rationalization and thought would lead to the birth of philosophy, and as a result, relationship would be replaced with the murkiness of religious ideology. Factions, sects, denominations and cults would form as the children of God searched for what was lost. Man would elevate his own opinion above the instruction of the Father, all the while neglecting the fact that the pathway of obedience is the way home.

It was only "one little thing," but it separated man from his Creator and from the Creator's original intention for him. It fractured the perfect beauty of the relationship between the Father, the human race and the rest of natural creation. That one act of disobedience pushed man outside the realm of spiritual, emotional and physical satisfaction, and man has been seeking for what was lost ever since. One little thing. One little tree. One little piece of fruit in a heavenly environment of lush beauty and magnificent provision. One small exception to perfect obedience.

Before the fateful decision was made to disobey the father's one instruction, there were no barriers or fences or walls. His children had access to Him, as any child does to a true father, in pure and open communication, without thought to hide or omit any part of him or herself. There was nothing to be ashamed of. The method and substance of their communication was flawless. Man had to ask for nothing. Everything was provided according to the Father's perfect intention. Man had only to enjoy the peace of his Garden home and to give thanks to the One who provided it.

As you receive the blessing of these words, and as you contemplate your individual response, beware that the wind of the Spirit is going to blow away the covering from all that is hidden. If you truly desire the fullness of Garden life, every disobedient act must be revealed, confronted and submitted to the Father's authority. There can be no hiding in the bushes in some ridiculous attempt to conceal your disobedience and the resulting shame. There can only be bare confession and repentance. If separation from Yahweh was the result of an act of disobedience, it stands to reason that restoration of fellowship will be the result of obedience.

You must forsake all…

That "one little thing" must be acknowledged and surrendered. It must be brought down from its place of exaltation and laid low at the Father's feet.

You shall have no other gods before me…

The act of disobedience committed by Eve and Adam was an act of idolatry. They worshipped their own idea and placed their own agenda above that of the Father. They decided their way was better. They rationalized and concluded that, since everything else was good and permissible for their enjoyment, certainly it would not hurt to claim "one little thing" as their own. What harm could it cause? Surely they thought their status as Garden dwellers would not be jeopardized. Surely the intimacy of their relationship with the Father would not be ruined. Surely I can reserve *one* secret, *one* hidden sin, *one* sordid detail, *one* strain of selfishness!

If you are not ready to trade your best idea for the Father's words and pictures, shake this word off your spirit and move on to your next book. The Father is seeking only true worshippers, true sons and daughters with nothing hidden. There can be no idols behind the veils that hang over the sanctuary of your heart, no dirt under your proverbial rug, no monsters in your closet. Come naked and honest (He knows anyway!) and give Him what you have reserved for so long. Give Him long, consistent acts of perfect obedience, for in the giving lies freedom like your brother, Adam, knew when he worshipped at the Tree of Life.

VANESSA

In December of 2008 City of Refuge opened Eden Village, a redemptive housing program for previously homeless women and children. Between the hours of 9 a.m. and 2 p.m. you can find Vanessa working at Eden Village's front desk. A few months ago I interviewed Vanessa for StoryCorps, a non-profit organization that records conversations as a means of preserving the American experience. Selected StoryCorps recordings are played on National Public Radio, and all conversations are submitted to the Library of Congress. Allow me to share a little of my warm-up conversation with Vanessa:

Me: Vanessa, share with me a memory you have from childhood.

Vanessa (contemplative): Well, Jeff, I can't do that.

Me: Why?

Vanessa: Because I didn't have no childhood.

Me: What do you mean?

Vanessa: I mean, the earliest thing I remember is when I was about five years old and I would go into my momma's bedroom and she would be laid out drunk on the bed with some man I didn't know. I would take my momma by the arm and pull her outta the bed 'cause I knowed it wasn't right. That happened a lotta times. I figure that ain't no kinda childhood, so I just say I never had one.

Me: Why did your mother do those kinds of things?

Vanessa: She did it 'cause she loved the liquor. She was controlled by it. She didn't care 'bout nothin' else.

Me: What makes you say that?

Vanessa: Well, when I was 'bout ten she traded me to a man for a pint of liquor. She told me to go to the store with this man and bring her back a pint, and when we got back she told the man he could have me. We didn't have sex that day. We waited a couple of days, but we started havin' sex, and when I was twelve I had a baby.

Me: So, you have a child that is twelve years younger than you?

Vanessa: That's right, a daughter. She'll be about thirty-five now, but I don't know where she is.

Me: Was your father around when all this happened?

Vanessa: Yep, he was around off and on. When he found out I was pregnant, he told my momma to just go ahead and let the little b—ch have the baby.

Vanessa went on with the horror story of abuse, neglect, alcoholism, prostitution and cocaine addiction. Tears ran down her puffy cheeks as she recounted a life of injustice unlike anything I have ever heard. A few minutes into the interview, I looked hopelessly at the StoryCorps facilitator, gesturing my loss of aptitude with upturned palms. I was a pitiful, emotional heap of human flesh, and I could not speak without my voice quivering and breaking. With tears in her eyes, the facilitator attempted to help, but we were both lost. As if she knew our dilemma, Vanessa carried the conversation and brought us back to where we could breathe.

Me: What goals do you have for yourself now, Vanessa? What do you want to accomplish?

Vanessa: I tell you what my number one goal is, Jeff. I just wanna get my GED. If I can just get my GED, I'll be happy. I ain't never accomplished nothin' like that in my life and it would make me so proud. If I can get that GED, the man upstairs can just call me home. I'll be satisfied."

I want to build a twelve thousand square foot stone house on my land, complete with immaculate landscaping and paved driveways and sidewalks everywhere. I'm sick of dust. Vanessa just wants a high school equivalency certificate. I want to get my kids through college and sit on the porch of my stone house for the last fifteen years of my life, sipping raspberry tea and iced mocha. Vanessa just wants a GED. I want a Nissan 350 Z with no payment book attached. Vanessa, well, you know…

I once saw a gathering of hot air balloons and was fascinated by their beauty and the sense of freedom that characterized the activity. There is something noble about rising slowly above the earth and drifting without inhibition over one's problems and sadness. Balloon owners decorate the great orbs in bright, celebratory designs as if to shout to the earth that they have found a way to escape her soil and water prisons. From above, one views earth from an entirely different perspective, with a sense of freedom and a spirit of prospect.

When I look at Vanessa Cowans, I think of hot air balloons, and don't tell my wife but I think I love her. From the time she was born, Vanessa was chained to the ground, inhibited by circumstances over which she had no control. She could do nothing about the parents to whom she was awarded. She was not the author of the poverty and destitution into which she was born. Vanessa was a victim of physical, mental, emotional and sexual abuse, and grasped the only painkillers available to her, drugs and alcohol. So many chains connected to so many sand bags, all pinning her to the dirty ground of her dirty world. But when the opportunity came, Vanessa began to shake off the chains and break loose from the weights that held her down. She embraced the Truth as it was presented and gobbled up the love of her new found family. She gladly followed the counsel of ministry leaders and found freedom in trusting someone else's judgment.

Vanessa was a spiritual corpse when she came to City of Refuge. She was cold and uninviting, like a building abandoned after a devastating storm. The debris of poverty, physical maladies, anger manifested in grenade-like explosions, insecurity and low self-esteem covered her life like fall-out from a volcano. She had an eleven year-old son she was prohibited from seeing. She was wandering through life with no perception of purpose, much less progress toward it. Vanessa was just passing hours in anticipation of the end, corpse-like, but she was willing to do anything to live again.

Oh yes, the dead may live again! The abandoned corpse, left rotting and foul, can be re-occupied by the Spirit of life. You are not unresurrectable. You have not gone too far! Your journey may have led you to bow at the tree of self-dependence, and you may find yourself hanging by the neck from that same tree, and your hearing and vision may be damaged or polluted, but YOU MAY LIVE! You may be hanging by no fault of your own. You may have been abused, neglected, rejected or led astray by someone you trusted, but the Father loves you as much as He loves anyone, and He wants to give you His life.

Vanessa, and many more like her, is a living testimony that a person can dwell in the middle of the angry fallout of human disobedience and still enjoy daily the fullness of the Father's Peace, Power, Provision and Protection. She lives in a small apartment in Atlanta's worst neighborhood, a quarter mile from City of Refuge. On her way to the warehouse each morning she passes monuments to people who were slain on the sidewalk for ridiculous reasons: Drugs, money, jealousy, competition, pure meanness. A few days ago a petty crack dealer was shot in the back right outside the warehouse fence. He bled out and died and is now memorialized by a life-sized, blow-up Spider Man doll and a Tickle-Me-Elmo. The man's demise is a sad, ironic paradox because he was never meant to die at all, much less shot down in the street like a disgusting rat, and certainly not destined to be commemorated by cartoon characters.

Vanessa's neighborhood is best known for its statistical afflictions. Her zip code is number one in Georgia for violent crimes, illegal drug activity, prostitution, high school dropouts, single parent households, inmates in the correctional system, and the list goes on and on. For many years Vanessa allowed the inheritance of disobedience to govern her life, and she stooped to remain aligned with its misery. Fact is the course of Vanessa's life was seemingly set when she was conceived. Poverty sat on her purpose, smothering it like a pillow over the face of a helpless child. Selfishness was passed on by the adults in her life, settling on her spirit and blocking the view of others and their needs. Addiction and perversion are the most prevalent and memorable monsters of her childhood.

When Vanessa came to City of Refuge she had no idea what to do. One could instruct her to assume a life of perfect obedience to the Father, but she had no perception of what it meant or how to proceed. The language of the Kingdom – purpose, destiny, service, grace, redemption, etc. – meant nothing to her. One may as well have spoken Chinese, and to my knowledge, Vanessa does not speak Chinese. She settled in the emergency shelter, believing that a roof over her head and food for her stomach was why she was here. The name of the game was survival. Do what it takes to see the sunset, then do what it takes to see the sunrise the following morning. This is just another homeless shelter, right? This is just another program designed to cleanse the city of its human refuse. This is just another rickety bunk situated in a row of rickety bunks, each bearing the lingering smells of previous survivors. This is just another brown sack, complete with bologna sandwich and all the fixin's, junk food for people with diabetes, high blood pressure, heart issues and a host of other problems. Right?

Wrong! Upon her arrival at City of Refuge Vanessa began to notice differences from the places she had been. The facility was clean and attractive. The sheets smelled fresh and the residents were required to make their beds and do chores. She began to hear the words "passion" and "excellence" and learned that these words were benchmarks of COR operations. Although the ministry went through its early years passing out the aforementioned sack lunches (and certainly a bologna sandwich is better than nothing, maybe), meal quality evolved into the best Vanessa had ever been part of. She began to attend Bible study classes conducted by Pastor Tony and others and soon began to connect the spiritual dots. The efforts of the ministry toward homeless people were acts of service in the Kingdom of God, and if one was going to represent the Kingdom of God in the earth and perform acts of service in obedience to the King's instructions, he should do so with "passion" and "excellence." Of course!

Vanessa knew she was tired of living as she had been for forty-four years, but she had never known there was a different way. Little did she know that the spiritual ghetto was not her only option, but that a lush garden filled with the Father's Peace, Power, Provision and Protection lay just down the pathway of obedience.

Vanessa Cowans did not come to the City of Refuge emergency shelter for women because she was on a quest to realize God's original intention for her. She just wanted a warm bed and a brown sack of "goodies." Little by little she began to sense there was something better. When she was moved from the shelter into stable housing, a little of the rubbish was removed. When groups of caring individuals would show up with good food, household gifts and lots of hugs, something shifted in Vanessa's spirit and hope began to spring up. When roommates, COR staff persons and Mission Church family members treated her like a sister instead of an item, understanding was birthed and she transformed before our eyes. As true sons and daughters of the Father walked in obedience to His instruction to bless "the least of these," this precious daughter, who was created in the image of her Father and intended to dwell in the Peace of Garden life, developed a new perspective and began her own journey of obedience.

Recently, I scolded my seven year old son, Riley, for cramming toys under his bed rather than putting them away properly. His response was, "But Daddy, you didn't tell me where to put them, you just told me to clean up!" My response was, "But Riley, you know the right way to do it. You know what I expect!"

In other words, Riley knows my heart. He knows my expectations and is fully aware of the consequences if those expectations are not met. From the time he came wriggling out of his mother on a marvelous September day in 2002, he has received my love, attention, Provision and Protection. This little boy's heart and spirit are intricately connected to mine and he recognizes my voice and connects it with love *and* authority.

Vanessa had no such blessing as a child. Her biological father gave her his blood and not much more. He was just a guy who periodically slept with her mother and considered it a curse each time the experience resulted in pregnancy. Children were a hardship, thus becoming the objects of his bitterness and resentment. It was not until she came to City of Refuge and began to attend church at The Mission that Vanessa learned someone truly loved her with a genuine, family-style love, and the love was not just proclaimed verbally but was lavished on her at every turn through acts of compassion and demonstrations of service. She also learned that the Father had placed spiritual authorities in human form in her life, and that obedience to them equated to obedience to Him. Although she was completely ignorant of the processes of hearing the voice of the Father and responding in obedience, she learned that the right people had been placed in her life to show her what to do. Like a thirsty sponge, Vanessa absorbed this and other powerful lessons and her personality began to change. Sad eyes began to sparkle and harsh language mellowed. To put it in Biblical terms, Vanessa's dark midnights became joyful mornings and her mourning became dancing.

"See that man right there" Vanessa says to visiting groups as she points to Pastor Bruce. "That man saved my life." Vanessa has broken the chains and soars in freedom above circumstances that once plagued her. She looks down on the cemeteries of her past where rotting corpses that chose a different road lie in their tombs or hang from majestic trees. She floats over poverty, anger, fear, addiction, disappointment, bitterness and hatred. She sees serpents in the grass below, remembering the plans they laid for her, but rejoicing in the awareness that serpents cannot fly!

"Daddy, can I get twenty dollars 'til my check come in?" Vanessa asks Pastor Bruce.

"I was waiting for that question" he responds lightly. "It is the 25th of the month. You're running a little late."

"In that case, make it fawty!" He hands her two twenty dollar bills, and they both laugh like children.

THE DREAM

Recently, I dreamed a police officer came to my door and asked me to accompany him to the neighboring house. As I walked onto my porch, I saw numerous patrol cars, ambulances and crime scene vehicles parked on the yard and street. The house next door reminded me of childhood trips to visit my grandparents in West Virginia – brown shingled walls and tin roof, coal dust dirty. The officer took me to the dwelling's front door and motioned me to enter. He remained behind, offering no instruction or counsel.

The interior of the building could have been any one of a dozen churches I remember from my youth. The old, country shotgun sanctuary was outfitted with wooden pews, floors and walls. The lights were off and it seemed I was alone. I saw the faint outline of a platform with small choir loft and giant pulpit. A communion table with two brass offering plates stood on the floor in front of a shadowy altar rail. I proceeded cautiously down the center aisle, not knowing what I was looking for, and still wondering if I was being implicated. To the right of the pulpit was an upright piano, and for a moment it seemed I could hear Sister Carol plunking out *Keep on the Firing Line*. She didn't play piano; rather, she plunked it in a manner that sent the melodies home with you where they would lodge and live for the rest of your natural life.

My eyes adjusted to the dimness and I continued my slow trek, contemplating a church next door to my home that I never knew was there. The militant Christian tune subsided, and when I got to the third row of pews, I froze. Something invisible made me know I should stop. Something called me without the use of language, like a child who knows it's time to go home even before he hears his mother's voice. My eyes were drawn to the right and I stooped to see the body of a young man lying on the floor near the wall, his head under the second pew and his feet stretched to the third. He lay on his side with his face toward the wall, but I knew him. I had seen that long, lean frame many times, and the thick, brown hair was not unfamiliar. I knew him and I knew his condition. He had chosen this place to die; he had chosen this kind of death. There was no sign of struggle and the body was past the stage of rigor mortis. It lay softly and peacefully on the wooden planks. It was a voluntary death.

Like rapidly ascending from a hole in the ground, I awoke from the dream with a cold knot in my stomach and a tear in the corner of my eye. For two days I wondered if the dream was prophetic, wondered if I should expect some horrible news that the young man, someone I know and cherish, had suffered an untimely death. Then the answer came: He is dead already. He walks, laughs, drives and pets his dog, but he is very, very dead. The symbolism became clear. He is spiritually dead and lying a corpse in the stale, dark sanctuary of his perverted religious ideals. He despised his blessings so long and added his own ingredients to the Truth recipe until the combination became spiritually lethal. When man elevates himself above his Creator, he digs his own proverbial grave. The young man was so close to life, freedom and fulfillment, but had chosen to make his spiritual heritage the tabernacle of his demise.

Around the world you can walk into sanctuaries that were once dedicated to worship, evangelism and discipleship, and see corpses, even skeletons sitting in the dark corners of their worn out religions, waiting for Carol to plunk or the preacher to massage but doing nothing to impassion their own relationships with the Father, and nothing about injustice outside the shingled walls. It is more than tradition or procedure alone that we tote the bodies of the dead to church for their final remembrance and commission. It is sadly symbolic that many churches are nothing more than morgues that house the remains of decaying religious ideals that long ago lost any semblance of life. But there is hope! Regardless of the circumstances of our spiritual deaths, we can live again. We can live as individuals and corporate bodies can be resurrected as well. In the beginning, there was formlessness, chaos and darkness. The Father's words brought structure, order and light. He formed man from the dust of the ground and breathed into his nostrils the breath of life, thereby imparting to man both physical and spiritual life. Individually and corporately, we can live again. Hope remains for the young man in the dream and hope remains for you. The Father still breathes and His breath still raises dusty carcasses from the ground and makes them into sons. Sons who walk in perfect obedience to His words are full of life and promise. The after-effects of my dream evolved from hollow dread to confident hope. I knew this young man was not beyond hope and I had utmost reliance that he would live again. I began to pray diligently for him. Recently, I have received reports that signs of life are being manifested in the young man. He is beginning to twitch, so I am intensifying my prayers. One day he will rise up and run like pre-fall Adam!

I believe.

WHERE ARE MY SONS?

Where are my sons and why have they forsaken me? Why do they not sit at my table and break bread, or stand shoulder to shoulder to help me push the plow? They do not join the fight against my enemies; rather, they have adorned themselves with the colors of my foes and placed the medallions I despise around their necks. They have taken up arms against me. If I turn my face to the east, they gaze west. If I lift my chin to the sky, they cast their eyes to the ground. If I proclaim the Truth, they go in search of a murmuring voice that contradicts my words. They wrap their arms around deceit and give it nurture until it becomes truth in their own minds. Oh my God, where are my sons?

What happened to the seeds of fatherhood I planted in the soil of their tender hearts? Were they burned up or strangled by thorn bushes or stolen away by treacherous birds? What happened to my dream of a thick stream of family blood running through life's valleys unhindered, unpolluted and unstopped by outside forces, for there is no force stronger than blood, right? But the sons of my dreams have left their security and broken the bond of blood and drank from pools filled with pestilence. They scoff at the blood stream and despise their blessings – they mock my name and deny my God. They sleep with whores in the gates of the temple and intoxicate themselves in the shadow of the altar of worship. Oh my God, where are my sons?

Children are an heritage from the Lord, but what is a man to do when the heritage is sold for the price of self-gratification? What is he to do when the birthright becomes less valuable than soup and the coat of arms good for nothing but jesting? A man raises sons to work the fields with him, to build their city and feed their flocks, yet they abandon him and he is left to endure the sun alone and to labor in solitude. He breaks his back to raise an eternal house with timbers of integrity, a roof of honor and a foundation of morality, while they construct paper shacks and ignite their efforts by their own foolishness. Oh my God, where are my sons?

I can only hope and believe the road they travel, with its bends and turns, distractions and dark places, will eventually loop around the valley of destruction and dead end at the road that leads home. And I will sit on the porch with my eyes to the road and will recognize their bent and ragged frames in the distance, weary from wandering and foul from the pig pens of their past, and I will softly declare, Oh my God, there are my sons.

LICENSE TO KILL

"Nothing counts so much as blood. The rest are just strangers." From the movie *Wyatt Earp*, 1994

"Then the Lord said to Cain, 'Where is your brother Abel?'

'I don't know,' he replied. 'Am I my brother's keeper?'

The Lord said, 'What have you done? Listen! Your brother's blood cries out to me from the ground'" (Genesis 4:9&10).

Harold Rockmore is somebody's son. I do not know if Harold's parents are still living, but each of us remains the child of his or her parents even after their departure. It would be difficult to track Harold's ancestry. He is from Jamaica and I wouldn't know where to start, and other than the satisfaction of curiosity, I'm not sure what would be accomplished by the discovery. Some would say that to know something of his past may help us understand why Harold has lived a life of deceit, rebellion and lawlessness, but in the end, does it really matter? Either way Cecil is still dead and Harold will still live out his days in prison. Harold Rockmore murdered Cecil Barnes, a transient laborer from somewhere in Alabama, because he had a license to kill.

I don't know the circumstances of Harold Rockmore's upbringing. I think he said he was born in Kingston and spent the first thirty or so years of his life there. It is probable he grew up in poverty because a large percentage of Jamaicans do, especially in Kingston's slums, but as a relatively young man he found the means to come to America. Perhaps he was chosen for a government work program or selected as a farm helper. Many Jamaicans once immigrated through such programs, but I am not sure about Harold. For all I know he could be here illegally. He could have come on a temporary visa and never went back.

Likewise, I don't know what makes Harold's heart dark and wicked. Perhaps when he was a child his mother abandoned him, resulting in separation anxiety disorder (SAD, for short) or some other horrible psychological anomaly. Could be his father beat him or burned him with cigarettes or exposed him to drugs and alcohol when he was very young. Maybe, when he was a teenager, he connected with the wrong crowd and was influenced by terrible opinions and exposed to rebellious behavior. Or maybe none of those things happened. I don't want to be guilty of implicating innocent people. Harold may have had marvelous parents and friends who had nothing to do with his bad choices. I just don't know.

I remember the times when Harold was happiest. There was the day he ate his lunch at Safe Haven and moved to a different table to try and get a second serving. Ryan, our "bouncer," calmly informed him we could not serve him twice or we would be obligated to serve everyone twice. After five minutes of twisting, lying and posturing, Harold declared he would see Ryan in hell, and that he would turn every table in the place upside down. He threatened to cut a few throats and splatter a few brains on the sidewalk. Of course, each threat was charged with a multitude of the most egregious words in the English language and all said with an enormous grin on Harold's face. He then got on his bike and rode off like he was headed to a church picnic. He seemed genuinely gratified and content.

Then there was the time I was walking to the dumpster and encountered Harold circling the cars in the front parking lot as if he was hired security. I knew he was looking for valuables to steal but I played it off because, frankly, I was alone and a little uneasy. I said weakly, "Hey Dred, you know when lunch is over you can't just wander around the parking lot. We'll see you on Thursday." He completely ignored my subtle implication and instead offered a question on a different subject. "Preacher, when you going back to Jamaica?" Harold had been in Atlanta for more than twenty years but still maintained a heavy Caribbean accent and it seemed to intensify when he spoke of things related to his homeland. This contributed even more to his menacing demeanor, but I saw the question as a chance to connect with him, to perhaps break through the barricades and communicate with civility, perhaps even become friends. As he waited for my answer, Harold's black eyes drilled holes through my chest and his benchmark expression, an evil grin that teetered between smile and smirk, made it difficult for me to think and respond.

I finally replied, "As a matter of fact I am going in two weeks. You should come go with me!" I chuckled lightly but the chuckle was quickly beaten back into silence when Harold's smile/smirk evolved in a nanosecond into much more smirk than smile.

"I can't go back there" he stated resolutely, "but how 'bout bringing me back some of that good Jamaican weed." The comment was followed by a chuckle of his own, but one not born of any warm attempt at becoming my buddy. It caused a shiver to run down my spine. I concluded that neither my love for Jamaica nor my familiarity with this man's native land and people was going to lead to a cozy relationship between us. The tone of his words implied there were things or people or situations in Jamaica that would make his return impossible and I suspected the scenarios probably included dead bodies. Harold Rockmore had a license to kill and there was no doubt in my mind he had used it.

At another particularly eventful Safe Haven lunch, I witnessed Harold unplug and pocket a cell phone an elderly lady from the neighborhood was charging in a wall outlet. In an attempt to not garner too much of Harold's attention for myself (I'm not the selfish type), I reported it to Pastor Bruce and let him handle it. Previously, I had informed Bruce and other staff members of my discernment that Harold had the capacity for murder, and given the chance he would not mind killing *me*. We all laughed at the thought, albeit nervously.

Harold was a man determined to get what he could get, manipulation and betrayal notwithstanding. The Mission had cared for him in hours of great need, but he seemed impervious to the usual impact of good deeds. In the spring of 2008 he was shot in the leg and nearly died. As if invincible, Harold had stolen a stash of drugs from two dealers and boasted about it on the streets. The thugs hunted him down, dragged him into an abandoned house and fired a .45 caliber slug into his thigh. They left him to bleed to death but he somehow got out and got the attention of passersby. Critical care personnel at Grady Hospital saved his life, but when he was released he had nothing and came directly to City of Refuge. We provided food, clothing and medication for several weeks. I stopped paying for prescriptions when I discovered he was selling the pain killers on the street, but we continued to bless Harold in practical ways and hold him up in prayer. We made sure he knew we were his family and we were there for him.

But Harold continued to despise his blessings and betray the Lord's commitment to him through us. Betrayal is always the hardest part to handle. When Harold was caught stealing the phone his reaction once again revealed what was in his heart – malevolence and murder. He was just looking for a reason, a method, a chance. He threatened to cut out our hearts, blow our heads off and rape every woman on the property. I am leaving out Harold's colorful adjectives in case my Mother reads this story. He warned us to be careful outside the COR gates, that he would see one of us at some point and leave our blood on the sidewalk. Pastor Bruce declared we had no choice but to ban him from the property. After another few minutes of ranting and threatening, Harold rode his bike slowly toward the gate, circling and smiling, avowing that he would see us later.

One of the most foreboding elements of our existence as human beings is our power to choose. Father could have created us as pre-programmed robots that function according to a standard that was already determined; however, He made man with a free will and the ability to rationalize, and with these components came the power of choice. After all, man was created in God's image and after His likeness, and Father certainly has the power to will and choose. From the beginning, Yahweh set before man the model for success as humans on this earth, but placed in man's hands and hearts the option to accept or reject it. The same loving Father who asked obedience of Eve and Adam, only to be disappointed by their choice and the promised results, asks of each of us the same thing, that we live in obedience to His words and reject the notion that we can raise ourselves to levels of self-sufficiency and accomplish the desired end.

Following their expulsion from the Garden, Eve and Adam still had choices. Each day they could choose to repent of their wrongdoing and renew their dependence on their Creator. Each day they could exercise purity of thought, attitude and deed. Each day they could acknowledge Father's authority and align themselves to receive His words and pictures. By their own choices they were condemned to live with the results of their disobedience. They had to labor for their food, find protection from bad weather and wild beasts and deal with pain and sickness; however, they still had the chance to experience Father's Peace, Power, Provision and Protection. As they wrestled with the problems they had exacted upon themselves, and as was the case before the "fall," what was required was obedience.

Eventually, Eve and Adam had children and the power of choice was passed on to them. From the time they were old enough to possess understanding the boys had witnessed the choices of their parents and had enjoyed the benefits of good ones and suffered the fallout of bad ones. Surely their mother and father shared stories about their previous life in the Garden. Surely they taught their sons the importance of listening to Father and following His instruction to the letter. I can't imagine they would not tell their sons how good life could be if they only remained obedient and how difficult things become when one chooses his own path. Isn't it part of our responsibility as parents to warn our children of the peril that can accompany bad choices? After all, Father had sufficiently warned them.

Of course, none of us knows exactly how Eve and Adam handled parenting. Unfortunately, most of the stories we find in Scripture are skeletal and leave out most of the details. What we can conclude is that when the boys were grown they were afforded the same opportunity as their parents to choose obedience or disobedience. Their lives began differently from that of their mother and father. They were born outside the Garden with all its blessings and were immediately presented with the by-products of their parents' failures. As they got older they had to work to eat and found it necessary to bring sacrificial offerings to Father as a means of worship and as penance for sins. They did not have immediate access to Him as their parents had in the Garden; rather, they had to meet requirements and perform service. Father was still there and still desired closeness with His children, but their choices were as imperative as ever.

Through the story of Cain and Abel, Father teaches us powerful lessons about His heart. He teaches us the significance of sacrifice and how important it is to know Him well enough to know what kind of sacrifice He desires. He teaches us that even when we mess up and bring the wrong sacrifice, or no sacrifice at all, He still loves us and gives us second (and third, fourth, fifth...) chances, and will still show us how to please Him. He reveals to us how essential our commitment to each other is and how we have a responsibility to "keep" our brothers in every sense of the word. After the cataclysmic act of disobedience in the Garden God did not give up on His children; rather, He re-established and re-emphasized the importance of obedience as the means to right relationship with Him and consistent enjoyment of His Peace, Power, Provision and Protection.

Cain and Abel each brought a sacrifice to the Lord, sacrifices they thought would please Him and produce favor. They had worked hard and gathered the best they had to offer. Cain brought fruits of the soil and his brother fat portions of meat. As we know, Father preferred meat to fruit and therefore looked more favorably on Abel's offering. Cain's reaction was a natural one. He became angry and jealous and as the Scripture indicates, "...his face was downcast" (see Genesis 4:5).

At this point Father teaches Cain a valuable lesson about choices. He does not condemn the young man for his offering. I am convinced that Cain could have shaken off his second place finish in the offering contest, learned a great lesson about the heart of Yahweh, and brought a fabulous offering next time. The indication is that Father was looking for such a reaction. He wanted the boy to learn something from the experience and exercise obedience to what he had learned. He wanted a great lesson to be extracted from the experience by both boys and by the rest of us who would come after them. My paraphrase of Father's response to Cain's anger is as follows: Why are you so upset? Why are you scowling and fuming that your brother did something that was more gratifying to me than what you did? I can almost hear Father adding muscle to that skeletal story and saying, Why don't you rejoice with your brother and just do better next time? Now that you know what I prefer, why don't you give thanks for a lesson learned and begin to plan to wow Me with your next offering? You can still do something good! You can put this behind you and move on! Don't be angry. If you make a good decision (a RIGHT decision) now, you will be accepted and everything will be ok. But I see sin crouching at your door and if you listen to the wrong voice you will be overrun by the results of your choice. You have to take control of your emotions and listen to me!

Unfortunately, Cain's eyes had been covered by a veil as he allowed his anger to become hatred and hatred to produce a seed of murder. His ears had been clogged by pollution born of selfishness and jealousy. He refused to hear and obey the words of Yahweh and chose to follow his own idea as it was fueled by the voice of the serpent. He formulated a plan to destroy his brother; thus, the first recorded act of bloodshed and murder took place. The table was set for brothers to war against brothers and for man to assume responsibility for the most critical of all choices, the choice to shed the blood and end the life of his own flesh. Father warned us that the "knowledge of good and evil" was more than we could manage and that it would present to us a world filled with destruction and death. But Cain chose it anyway and many of his descendants follow the same pattern today. Through Cain's choice we were issued a license to kill and the blood of many, many brothers cries from the ground.

After the murder Father confronts Cain and presents to him a question: "Where is your brother, Abel?" In a story that is missing so many details, I believe Cain's answer is recorded as a means of issuing to all mankind one of the most important lessons in the Bible. He responds to God's question with a question of his own. "Am I my brother's keeper?" I do not want to be charged with presuming to speak for the Almighty, but knowing Him as well as I do I am sure He won't mind if I speak for Him this one time and add a little more muscle to the skeleton:

OF COURSE YOU ARE YOUR BROTHER'S KEEPER, CAIN! ARE YOU KIDDING ME?! I placed the two of you together to love, support and protect each other. You both have the same blood, and it is My blood, and it carries within its cells a link between you and me and each other that should not be violated. His blood should have been equal in priority to your own, not a useless substance to be spilled on the ground beside the dung of animals. You have listened to the wrong voice, Cain, and made an awful decision. Each brother has an obligation to the other, and all brothers to each other. The obligation is to stand shoulder to shoulder and defend each other from the enemy's attacks. It is to share your bread with him when he has none. It is to give to him a coat and shoes from your closet when his are tattered. It is to visit him when he is sick or in prison and to give him shelter when he is homeless. Your obligation is to cheer when he receives recognition and mourn when he is downtrodden. He breathed the same breath as you and it is My breath. Cain, you have stolen my authority and declared yourself qualified to do my job. You have become your own god. You have followed in the footsteps of your parents and usurped authority that is not rightfully yours. Now your brother's blood cries to Me from the ground, "Am I my brother's keeper?" What a ridiculous question!

Harold Rockmore sat on his bicycle at the corner of Lowery and Jett with his dredlocked head cocked back, feet spread wide to balance the bike and the usual expression adorning his brown face. His eyes moved constantly, back and forth, up and down, here and there. They did so because Harold was always looking for opportunities – an unlocked building or car door, a cell phone left unattended, a gap near the front of the feeding line. He was a schemer, manipulator, deceiver and liar. It was a way of life. Harold was rotten, and he had a license to kill.

When he saw the City of Refuge bus coming down Lowery the smile/smirk on Harold's ragged face widened and his black eyes seem to sparkle. I light up when the waitress places a perfectly grilled ribeye and steaming baked potato in front of me, or when my little boy runs to the door and jumps into my arms when I get home from work. Harold beams at any opportunity to make trouble or spread fear. Such ventures seem to be his lifeline.

I was driving the bus and when I was a few yards away he raised his right hand in the air. Thinking he had gotten over his anger and vengeful attitude, I started to wave back, but suddenly he leveled his hand and extended the index finger toward me. Like a child playing cops and robbers, Harold simulated two gunshots, then dropped his hand and began to laugh and bob his head up and down in an affirmative nod. I did what any brave man would do. I pretended not to see him and sped up.

My discernment was right. Three days later Harold came to our Sunday morning feeding location, the liquor store parking lot at the corner of Bankhead and Lowery. Bruce banned him from the property but we have never forbidden anyone to eat at the street feedings. Harold got into an argument with another man in line. He was a quiet, muscular, hard working fellow from Alabama named Cecil. Names were called and threats were made, mostly by Harold. A shoving match ensued and one of our volunteers had to step between them. Another two days passed and Harold showed up at a job site where Cecil was working. As a means of provoking his perveived adversary, in plain sight he took a step ladder and walked off with it. Cecil followed him and demanded the ladder back. They argued again and a fight broke out. The fight was no contest because Cecil was much too big, strong and healthy for Harold to contend with. But, bruised and bleeding, Harold swore he would return to settle the score.

Within fifteen minutes he came back and shouted insults and threats from the edge of the property where Cecil was working. Cecil approached him and Harold walked away, down the alley toward Lowery. Ignoring counsel from his co-workers to disregard the troublemaker, Cecil followed and when Harold reached the end of the alleyway he turned and walked aggressively back toward his brother. In a swift motion that left Cecil no time to react Harold drew an automatic pistol from his belt and shot Cecil once in the center of the chest. Cecil staggered backwards into a light pole and slid down to the ground, settling at the bottom of the pole as if he was taking a break from work. Seventy-five minutes passed before anyone called 911. The other guys on the job site said they heard a noise but did not know what had happened. By that time Cecil's blood had joined the cry, spreading out on the dirt beneath him like a giant, crimson amoeba. Harold Rockmore had a license to kill and another brother must answer the Father's questions.

As I said before, betrayal is the hardest part. Whether you look on the next pew, across the street or across the ocean, the people you see are your brothers and sisters, each one a child of the same Father, created by His own hand and breathing His breath. "Am I my brother's keeper?" Of course I am! And I have no right to shed his blood! Radical, militant terrorists want to spill my blood. I feel betrayed more than anything else. But on a more personal level, I feel even more betrayed by Harold Rockmore, my brother from right here in Atlanta with whom I tried to share fellowship and break bread, but who wanted to kill me.

The early chapters of Genesis reveal our origin and tell us much about Father's intention and how the first human beings set a horrible precedent of disobedience. It seems God's children have never fully understood that the world's problems are a direct result of ignoring Father's plan in favor of our own. We continue to exalt our opinions above His Truth and to elevate our ideas against the knowledge of Him. We wear veils and seem very proud to do so. We throw around our opinions as if they are infallible while His Word lies dormant or falls on deaf ears. Throughout history mankind has experienced great favor and prosperity when he listens and responds in obedience to Father's instruction. This pattern began in the second chapter of Genesis when Yahweh created man in His own image and continues today. As long as Eve and Adam remained true to Father's sole mandate, they lived in the abundance of Garden life. Even though their children were born into a different environment, they were presented the same options: Do what is right and live in Yahweh's favor or disobey and live on your own. The same choice was there for Cain's descendants and has continued throughout history.

Following Cain's murderous mistake, in Genesis 4:26 we are told that "… men began to call on the name of the Lord." The descendants of Cain were given the same right to choose and surrounding the verse acknowledging their submission to the Most High there is no account of poverty, murder, immorality or any other form of evil, save one man who informs his family in verse 23 that he has killed a young man who wounded him. There is always someone who believes violence is a reasonable answer and another brother's blood joins the cry. The contrast is very clear – hear the Lord and obey His words and you will enjoy safe, peaceful, prosperous lives, or do your own thing and live with the resulting destruction and death.

In chapter 5 we find a list of descendants that lived long and seemingly peaceful lives. Perhaps they learned from their ancestors valuable lessons that affected their choices. We know some of them were very close to Father, and that can only happen through a life of obedience. As a matter of fact, Enoch walked so closely with God that Father just "took him away" (see Genesis 5:24). I'm not sure where he was taken to, but it wouldn't surprise me if it was a Garden where Peace, Power, Provision and Protection were abundant, and where the two of them could walk and talk in the cool of the evening.

Men like Enoch proved that Father's intention for His children has not changed and that each of us can walk with Him, and through our obedience enjoy the full benefit of true sonship. We still have a choice and it is our choice that dictates the ultimate success or failure of our lives. God is not the author of calamity, confusion, chaos, sickness, poverty and death. These result from the decisions of mankind to raise his own ideas against the knowledge of God. Once I was asked by a young man the following question: "If there is a God, and if He loves us, then why does He allow children to suffer and die?" The inference of the young man's question points the arrows of blame in the wrong direction. Suffering and death on all levels are the result of man's self-reliance and disobedience, not the will or negligence of our Creator.

If Eve and Adam had chosen obedience they would have continued to dwell in the safety and abundance of the Garden. If Cain had chosen obedience he would not have been expelled from his homeland and forced to wander the earth scraping and scratching to survive each day. In addition, he and his brother would have lived long, happy lives and enjoyed the closeness that brothers should. If the other descendants of God's first children (including Abel, had he not been murdered) had continued in obedience, they would have flourished in Peace and harmony, but we know that many chose their own path as well. By the sixth chapter of Genesis the earth is filled with greed, lust and selfishness to the point that Father grieves that He has made man and His heart is filled with pain. In verses 11 and 12 the earth is described as "corrupt and full of violence." Sound familiar? Father sees that man is absorbed in himself to the point "that every inclination of the thoughts of his heart was only evil all the time" (v. 5). Father is so brokenhearted at the way man has used his power of choice that He wants to wipe man from the face of the earth.

Even today we can get it right if we choose to. Imagine this: What if there was only one rule to follow (just like in the Garden), just one very simple rule. What if the rule was this: "Love the Lord God with all your heart, mind, soul, and strength, and love your neighbor as yourself" (Luke 10:27). If every individual on earth began to exercise this one simple principle on a daily basis, would the earth be a Peaceful place? Would the Power of Almighty God be manifested so that everyone can see and benefit? Would His Provision cover the earth and eliminate poverty and unnecessary suffering, as those with abundance share with those who have nothing? Would Protection be our reward as we no longer have to worry about being attacked, raped, robbed or terrorized by our brothers? What if obedience became the benchmark of human existence?

COFFINS AND FLOWERS
The Power of Choice

For the survivors a funeral is a picture of life's contrasts, a snapshot of the path we travel and the terminal of our choices. Encapsulated in one frame is the coffin, cold and unforgiving, uncomfortable regardless of the kind coloring or soft amenities, and the flowers, magnificent in their aura and therapeutic in their aroma. Perhaps the flowers are meant to buffer the reality of the coffin, perhaps simply to remind grieving observers that life is beautiful and aromatic but will eventually wither and bow.

It was with coffin and flowers set as ambiguous backdrops that I witnessed a miracle. The coffin's tenant had heard the beckoning voice of despair and died by his own hand. Life's path is lined on one side by coffins and on the other by flowers. Troy Douglas Johnson had walked among the coffins until they became the lone objects of his vision, and now his pallid countenance seemed one with their satin linings. Many who cared for Troy and his family sent flowers, and at the graveside these vivid tokens surrounded the coffin, the most lucid at the head and foot, and the grandest of all draped over the bronze box.

The atmosphere was typical of that which surrounds sudden and self-inflicted departure. There was the usual heaviness of grief borne on the faces and in the postures of loved ones and friends, accompanied by subconscious manifestations of sullen, almost angry confusion mixed with periodic enigmatic expressions of relief. This strange combination of human emotions produced an unsettled feeling, as when one awaits an impending storm.

The graveside service was brief – a standard set of Scriptures mumbled by the preacher, most of which related the fleeting uncertainty of life, the inevitability of death and the promise of a better life to come, followed by a prayer beseeching God's comforting presence for the family and a final quiet word and handshake for those on the front row. The family lingered for a moment, then slowly drifted from under the tent and began to mingle with other mourners, most migrating to pockets of comfort among familiar faces.

As a student of humanity I stood and absorbed the motions and mannerisms of individuals. There was Carolyn, the aunt, twenty years older than when we saw her five years ago and seemingly very proud of her progression. She wore a powder blue dress and white sweater, a gray bun pulled tight to the back of her head, and Reeboks on stocking feet. Her thin shoulders bent slightly forward as she chirped colloquialisms to those in her circle. She had grown comfortable with funerals.

Everyone else was subdued: Darrell, the brother, in dark glasses and black suit; Douglas, the father, with quavering voice, wondering aloud what recourse should follow his son's demise but to go back to work on Monday; a guy in a blue Dickie's shirt with *Tim* on the breast tearfully recounting Troy's record-setting golf cart assembly at the plant. It was a page from a Steinbeck novel, a wistful scene from a Bogart film. I resolved to leave with solid confirmation concerning my stolid opinions about mankind, that we are born and die, and between the two events lean heavily upon each other.

And then it happened. My watchful eye was drawn to a motion under the tent, and like leaving a dream to again face the reality of time and space I became aware of a small child turning cartwheels on the graveside carpet. He was between the front row and the coffin and was laughing and falling and talking to himself. His shirt tail hung ungracefully from under a green sweater vest and covered the top of corduroys that were twisted from his acrobatics. He bounced and giggled and called for his daddy to watch, but aside from my interest he was totally ignored. I wanted to summon the world to watch with me but I was sure they would not understand. I was learning powerful lessons and was torn between ecstasy and guilt that the moment was solely mine.

The mental lens that only a moment ago panned the crowd was now fixed on a small, solitary figure who was finding joy amid the tears, confusion and irony. He turned and faced the grave, and my breath caught as I thought of boys and dirt and inevitability.

He is fascinated by the coffin, I thought. Will he touch the handles or rub the glossy casing? Perhaps he will try to crawl under it to examine the freshly dug destination of Troy's remains.

I wondered if I should do something. I tried to sort through the possibilities for calamity or mishap and concluded that the greatest possible calamity would be to molest this moment with my interference. Though poised to act if necessary, I stood still and watched.

The boy stood with a posture of curiosity mixed with fascination, rocking slightly from side to side, swaying indecisively between coffin and flowers. As I knew he would, he began to move slowly forward. With the dubious steps of one traversing unfamiliar ground, he progressed, leaning nearer to his destination with each step. Suddenly it was obvious to his solitary witness that the child had no coffin in his eye or thought. He saw only flowers! He stopped at a generous spray of roses and carnations at the head of the box, and with untucked shirt and crooked corduroys leaned toward the fattest rose, burying his tiny nose among its petals. He clasped his hands behind his back, relying on no sense but smell to fully absorb this moment. He drew in all the air little lungs could hold and rocked back, releasing the breath slowly and mumbling, "Mmmm, dat 'mells good."

I wanted to laugh aloud, but it was a funeral and the coffin and its owner were the main attraction. One doesn't laugh when coffins are present, unless one is a little child. He went back to the rose for more and I was swept into a furious and conflicting current of feeling, now wanting to join the brown-eyed treasure in his moment of repose, now wanting to call the oblivious crowd to witness the scene, now wanting to remain still lest I should ruin things. I wanted to call for a re-do on the funeral and turn the preacher's benign platform into a flower garden, inviting Carolyn and Douglas and all others who still possess the power of choice to come out from among the coffins and bury their faces in life's rose petals.

I wanted to do all these things, but chose rather to watch in hopes of photographing the images with the camera of my mind and later transferring the pictures into words. But behind the words is a little boy who laughs and plays in the face of death, not intimidated by its inevitability, and teaches us all that life's path is lined with coffins and flowers, and the greater of these is flowers.

THE RECIPE
FROM FATHER TO SON

Jesus, my son, I am proud of you. I am proud of you because I always know where you are. You are always where you are supposed to be. When it was your time to sit among the elders, you were there. When the crowds were assembled to receive your words and touch, you were there. When the crowds went away and you were called to solitude, you found the appointed place to commune with me. When it was time to face the enemy, you never ran and hid but always stood with resolve and faced the challenge.

Jesus, you heard my words and put into practice what I said. You are a wise man. I told you the task would be difficult, but that it would exceed in importance all previous assignments given to men. I told you the path would be lined with bitter thorns and at times the journey would be dark and lonely, yet you walked in my power because you walked in obedience and you feared no evil. I told you the struggle would be so painful that I would be compelled to turn my face and that you would feel abandoned, and that it was alright to feel that way and to question but not to relent. The questions came (and that's ok) but you remained true to your purpose, and hope was reborn. I am proud of you. You are an obedient son.

Now you sit with me, for such is the result of loyalty and obedience. You are right where you are supposed to be.

The love of the Father is unconditional. He loves every man, woman, boy and girl on this planet. His love has been the same for every individual who has ever lived, and He will love equally those yet to be born. Believe it or not, God loves the hate-driven suicide bomber as much as He loves the grandmother who teaches Sunday School to toddlers in any American church. God loves people. We are still His highest creation and he reserves the deepest spot in His heart for us. He did not begin to despise Eve and Adam after their sinful act, nor has He ever hated a person because of his or her disobedience. God's love is immeasurable and unconditional as illustrated by His willingness to sacrifice Jesus for people who were disobedient and self-centered.

As Paul says in I Corinthians 13, three things remain – faith, hope and love. Perhaps the apostle was referring to the Father's attributes rather than those of man, for certainly there are people in whom faith is dead, hope has vanished, and love has dissipated. There are people with tremendous hatred in their hearts for other human beings, some with hatred for everyone, including themselves. Each day there are people around the world who commit suicide because they have lost all hope. The earth is certainly home to many individuals with no faith.

Though these holy attributes have been lost in the hearts of so many of God's children, they have remained in the heart of the Father. He has faith that His Kingdom will be established in the earth and His plan will be realized. He possesses hope that His children will return to Garden life to dwell with Him for eternity. He has immeasurable, unconditional love for you and me, and nothing can change that.

With these thoughts in mind, we are sometimes guilty of viewing unconditional love as the dominant theme of the relationship between God and man, when it is not. God loves His children. He loved Eve and Adam and all that followed, right up to you and me. He loves pastors and prostitutes, teachers and terrorists, leaders and liars, tongue talkers and drug traffickers; however, God's love for us does not determine our spiritual success. Obedience to His words does. Though every human being receives the same measure of His love, some respond in obedience to the instruction and some do not. It is the level of obedience that each of us exercises that leads to spiritual success or failure. Some choose to embrace the Father's mandate to hear and obey, and others choose their own way. In other words, there are two paths, the path of obedience and the path of disobedience. His way or our way, and our way always leads to separation. Lucifer chose his own way and was removed from Heaven where the presence of God dwelled. Adam and Eve chose their own way and were expelled from the garden where intimacy with the Father was a way of life. Cain chose his own way and was driven from his homeland where the Father's provision was plenteous. Throughout history millions of others have chosen, and continue to choose, their own way, thereby separating themselves from the Peace, Power, Provision and Protection afforded by a lifestyle of obedience.

Jeff Deel

Isaiah said, "All we like sheep have gone astray. We have turned every one to his own way, and the Lord has laid on him the iniquity of us all" (Isaiah 53:6). To turn to our own way leads to iniquity and Holy Spirit will not share space with iniquity. One's own way is the sinful way, the disobedient way, and though the Father still loves us our disobedience creates separation between Him and us. He loves us enough to "lay on him (Jesus) the iniquity of us all," but the requirement of obedience remains. He loves us enough to extend grace upon grace upon grace, which allows us to return to Him regardless of how many times we fall (e.g. Jonah, David, Simon Peter, the prodigal son). In each of these cases, the disobedient child came back to the Father with a repentant and submissive spirit, willing to obey what they heard, but the time of their rebellion was characterized by separation.

The world has serious problems and many people choose to challenge the precepts of Christianity by asking why a loving God would allow such terrible things to happen. Why do children die tragically? Why are there so many natural disasters? If God is love, why does He allow his people to suffer from devastating diseases? Why is there so much chaos and turmoil? At the risk of over-simplifying the world's problems, the answer to each of these questions is the same: God isn't to blame for these things. MAN IS. Evil was introduced to the world through the disobedience of man, and throughout history man has continued to complicate his problems by living in a pattern of disobedience and self-reliance. We continue to make our "own way," yet we blame the results on Him. Eve and Adam, the guilty parties in the Garden tragedy, suffered greatly for their disobedience, but they were not the only ones. Their children and grandchildren suffered as well and the same pattern has repeated itself throughout history. Men still commit selfish acts of disobedience and the guilty, as well as the innocent, still suffer the consequences.

God's love is real, and it is true that He loved us enough "...in that while we were yet sinners, Christ died for us" (Romans 5:8). However, had we not *been* sinners this supreme act of love would not have been necessary at all. We would still be living the Garden life. In other words, we started it! God's love for His children has always been part of the equation. It was not until man decided on his "own way" that the problems began. The Father continues to love us in spite of our behavior but does not remove the results. As long as we choose sin the horrible effects will plague our lives.

The Father sent Jesus to earth to die as a sacrificial lamb, thereby providing the opportunity for atonement to his disobedient children. But there was and is more to Jesus' purpose for living here. Between the time of His arrival in a stable in Bethlehem and His ascension back to the Father, He provided powerful, hope-filled information that, if followed, leads to victorious life in his Kingdom, and it starts right here on earth. In the words of Jesus and in the example of His life are messages indicating the Father's heart toward us has not changed and that the fullness of garden life is still a possibility. In His instruction are keys that unlock the bounty of His Peace, Power, Provision and Protection. In Him is abundant life that is filled with hope and the expectation of our revelation as "true sons" of the Father.

So where do we start? Before I answer that question, allow me to share a personal testimony. A couple of years ago I visited a friend of mine, Doug, in Ohio and attended Sunday worship at the church he pastors. Following the service Doug introduced me to a lady and said he would like her to pray for me. I consented and the lady (I had never seen her before and have not seen her since) began a very generic prayer, but before long her words became much more passionate and personal. She began to pray for my children and to say things about them only family members or close friends would know. My interest grew as I realized the level of her spiritual insight, and I began to hang on her words. Toward the end of the prayer, she said the following (paraphrased):

Before you are four doors. You are to walk through these doors one at a time. You must focus on each one individually and walk through it before you consider the next one. The first door will be difficult to open, but you must press into it. You must work hard and persevere. Do not give up, for once you have pressed through this door the next three doors will swing open in succession.

I walked away from this experience confused and a little frightened because I did not really know what the message meant or what the doors represented, but I knew there was a decision before me. I could choose to ignore the words and allow skepticism to destroy their potential, or I could begin to seek for the first door and prepare my heart and mind for the task ahead. I chose the latter.

I now know that my trip to Ohio was not a coincidence. It was ordained of the Father so He could get my attention and so His words would not be drowned out by the familiar noises of my life. Before the trip I was feeling extremely dissatisfied and unfulfilled and was sensing that something had to change. In a fashion very untypical to me, I jumped on a plane and flew to Cincinnati, having informed Doug only a few days before that I was coming. It was a great weekend of fellowship, relaxation and good food. I had meaningful conversations with Doug, a man for whom I have tremendous respect and admiration. I can't remember most of what happened yesterday, but I remember his message that Sunday morning. He talked about times in our lives when we do not know what to do or what decision to make and we feel confused and frustrated. He reminded the congregation (especially me) that the Father has a plan and if we will remain faithful and walk in obedience it will pop up before us like a beautiful flower. It was there as a seed all along, just waiting for us to forsake our "own way" and to begin to take bold steps of obedience to His words.

You may be standing before a door and have no idea how to unlock it, or you may still be looking for the door. Regardless, here's where you start: You begin to listen intently for His voice and to respond in complete, uncompromised obedience to what you hear. You may begin by studying what He has already said. Dig into His word with ferocity. Read it over and over and over. Read it aloud. Put up a different Scripture each week on your fridge and as a wallpaper or banner on your cell phone and computer. Pray the Scriptures. Sing the Scriptures. After all, the written word of God is the most significant document in history. Why not allow it to be the most significant document in your life?

Next, do what it says! Be obedient to the words of Jesus Christ and your life will change. Though the weekend in Ohio was restful and fun, my obedience to what I heard while I was there was the key to everything. Had I gone with clogged ears and heard nothing, or had I heard and refused to obey, I would only be deeper in my personal pit of frustration and confusion. Obedience was everything. It still is.

One of the most powerful lessons Jesus taught during His time on earth was the lesson of the wise and foolish builders. Being the son of a pastor, I heard the passage read and expounded on in Sunday School lessons, sermons and devotionals dozens of times when I was young. As well, I have read and taught on the passage many times through the years. However, it was only recently that I really absorbed the true meaning of the teaching and thereby discovered the key to victorious Kingdom living. The key was lying right there the whole time, fully uncovered and ready to be used to unlock the doors to Peace, Power, Provision and Protection, and I had overlooked it my entire life. Ironically, it was in the first phrase of the passage: "Whoever hears these words of mine and does what I say…" (See Matthew 7:24-27).

WOW! Can it really be that simple? Is the key to building a spiritual life so solid that hurricanes and tornados cannot move it really that uncomplicated? Is it possible that everything else the Father has to say to His children is inextricably linked to those few simple words? The answer is yes!

If I spent the rest of my life with a notebook and pen, or behind a computer, I could not find the words to describe the impact the discovery of that precious key continues to have on me. It brought the greatest hope a man can know, that the realization of our God-given purpose is really possible. It transformed the commands of Scripture from results-driven laws to joy-filled assignments. It relieved the guilt associated with rejection of man made religious doctrine. It showed me that salvation is of imminent importance, but that a pathway of obedience lies beyond its beautiful gate, and that rejection of the pathway amounts to rejection of the salvation experience.

But perhaps most importantly, discovery of the key led me back to the Garden where I witnessed afresh what was lost when my most ancient of ancestors refused to hear and obey the Father's words and chose their own way. I have witnessed and contemplated the results of their disobedience and my spirit has teetered between pity, sorrow and anger. Though it happened so long ago, I have, at times, been consumed with regret that it happened the way it did. Garden life was our Father's intention for us, but my life is so often far from gardenesque. But the instruction of Jesus follows me to the Garden and there I hear it as an echo that began when His Father first commanded Eve and Adam to hear His words and respond in obedience. I see clearly that His intentions for us have not changed and that the key to realization of those intentions is still the same. "Whoever hears these words of mine and does what I say…" is not a new word for a new day – it is the same word that "in the beginning" stood as the foundation of the relationship between the Father and His children. It was profoundly re-emphasized through the life of Christ, the perfect model of obedience. He repeatedly made it clear that he came to accomplish the will of the Father, that is, to obey the Father's words.

Centuries have passed since Jesus walked the earth, but the foundation remains the same: Hear his words and respond in obedience and you are like a wise man who builds his house on a rock. The "rock" is obedience. In other words, the man who lives in a pattern of obedience establishes a firm foundation on which a house can be built that will stand against any storm. Refuse to hear, or hear and refuse to obey, and the integrity of the house is compromised because the foundation is unstable. No other part of the construction of the house can be trusted, no matter how well-planned or meticulously crafted, because the foundation is faulty. In such case, beware of storms.

I no longer trust my own judgment, and that decision has brought great Peace and freedom to my life. For most of us life's journey consists of parties and funerals, dancing on mountain tops and laboring through valleys as if we are dragging a piano behind us, bringing all accounts current with money left over and deciding which bills to leave unpaid. It is during the down times that our mettle is tested and our faith tried. Personally, I spent many years failing the tests and I have a feeling that many people reading this book have done the same.

People have stories and the stories deserve to be told. Along the way, I have met and worked with thousands of individuals, all of whom were created by the same loving Father that created you and me, and all of whom have been presented with the choice to follow His instruction or choose their own way. A few of the stories are included in this thesis on obedience to illustrate both paths. Though still battling life's trials and tribulations, some of them continue to align themselves to hear Father's words and strive daily to obey them, thus making themselves perpetual candidates for His Peace, Power, Provision and Protection. Others have chosen the path of self-reliance and continue to struggle with the results – poverty, imprisonment, guilt, confusion, frustration and even death.

This book is the first of four doors that I found it necessary to push through after my trip to Ohio. In my time of frustration and dissatisfaction, I stepped out of my box and allowed Father to give me His words. Most importantly, I decided to obey what I heard.

OLD HOMELESS MAN

He moves in slow motion, like dark brown molasses
and cannot recount the faces he passes
or paint a 'scape of the house on the corner
though locked in this birdcage since he was born
into colors all burnished and textures all stippled
sidewalks all wheelchair ramps for the crippled
A child chases butterflies – he chases breath
married to pain with a vision of death
All the people are gone he could call as his blood
hopes for tomorrow are drowned in the flood
of hunger and want and lonely despair
droplets of love turned to rivers of care
The smells haven't changed since the marchers came through
and dropped off a hope with a blanket of mildew
but feet are still beating a flat-footed trek
and life's blood pushes his heart to expect
that a better day will rise on the wind
maybe winter, or summer, no, winter again
So he walks with black eyes counting cracks in the cold
past an ancient survivor, but wait, she's not old
just the years are piled on more than one at a time
likely fifteen by the time she was nine
but how can he worry himself with her plight
when each moment for him is a life and death fight
like the skinny dog at the green store front
hungry for spoils, but too frail to hunt
So he lodges another day in the book
and settles in shadows away from the look
of the passersby gazing through tainted glasses
at the man who moves like dark brown molasses

EVOLUTION

1992

On a street corner on the Bankhead strip a young man sits astride his motorcycle. It is one of those lightning fast "crotch rockets" that often rips past unsuspecting motorists on the freeway with startling aggressiveness. He chats with his friends in language laced with street euphemisms and profanity, while young men wearing over-sized t-shirts and baggy jeans that sag below their narrow behinds strut by, and older people with hard faces step between and swing open the squeaky doors of the corner store. The young man is busy talking about Orlando and Miami and his "family" connections in Florida and how the "family" is taking care of business and the business is so much better than working at Sea World because you can make more money in an hour taking care of "family business" than you can make in a month at Sea World, or anywhere else twenty-one year old guys with only a high school education work.

He recently traveled from Orlando to Atlanta on a Greyhound bus with the six year old daughter of a "brother" in tow because the presence of a child usually evaporates suspicions, and since he was carrying a few kilos of cocaine, suspicion was something he could do without. "Man, you got to love whachoo do to ride a bus fifteen hours with a little kid" he jokes. They all agree that it's "trippin' but definitely worth it."

The young man is simply known as G and is quite familiar on the Bankhead strip as one of the "Miami boys," a group of drug runners who make regular trips back and forth to Florida to bring drugs to Atlanta. He was born Gregory Tyrone Washington into a military family in Houston, Texas, and during his early years was bounced between Houston and Los Angeles where his grandmother lived, eventually being victimized by his parents' divorce and moving to Orlando with his mother. She worked at a Disney World hotel and Gregory went to school and played sports until his junior year when he was accepted into a co-op that gave him a job and culinary training at Sea World. He was born with leadership skills and an entrepreneurial spirit, and these qualities immediately manifested themselves. Gregory worked hard to maintain his studies and excel as a trainee, always prompt and respectful, attentive and diligent.

At first Gregory was proud of the little paycheck he was handed each week. He was learning a trade and was being rewarded financially for doing so. There was not much left after taxes but it came in handy and made him feel important. His mother was proud. He was going to make something of himself. Her only son was walking the right path, staying out of trouble, making good decisions. Gregory had beaten the odds. He was a black kid from a broken family attending a public high school and living in the city. It is usually a design for disaster but her boy was going to be alright, so she thought.

The guys on the Bankhead corner are now drinking beer from cans tucked inside brown bags and deftly passing a joint among them. G is feeling good when he cranks the bike and rolls onto the street, checking the time on his watch because he has an appointment to deliver an ounce of powder to a client in Buckhead, and he knows tardiness makes people nervous and nervousness sometimes leads to bad decisions. He is careful to maintain the speed limit and obey all traffic laws. No need to give the APD something to get excited about. G rides past ratty old buildings with burglar bars on the doors and windows, liquor stores with smelly dumpsters decorating their parking lots, soul food joints and little shops with signs in the windows announcing: *Food Stamps Welcome.* He makes good money on these streets, much better than he would ever have made as a chef or restaurant manager.

Gregory first saw a stack of hundred dollar bills when he was still in high school and was working long hours to get a diploma and bring home a few dollars from Sea World. The boy carrying the wad of bills had no job and had already dropped out of school, but he had found a way to get rich without going through the process and to Gregory the idea bore a romantic attraction that almost immediately turned to obsession. He had been toying with the idea of joining the Navy and continuing to learn and advance, but isn't money the ultimate goal anyway? He thought, *If I can make enough to pay my bills, have nice things and retire comfortably, isn't that what everyone wants? Why should I spend years making a pauper's wages and struggling like so many people I know when I can have it now?* The questions arose in conversations with his buddies and swam through his mind when he was alone. With his work ethic and people skills he could be rich in no time.

Bankhead to Buckhead – a tale of two cities. They are only a few miles apart but the contrast is stark. At night Buckhead is bright and the tall buildings that house law firms, marketing outfits and financial institutions produce a sense of dignity and grandeur, unlike the squat houses and stores of G's side of town. But there are druggies in Buckhead as well, maybe a little more sophisticated and perhaps using money earned in professional endeavors rather than from prostitution, theft or gifts from the government, but druggies nonetheless. G doesn't mind riding to the clean part of town. Money is money no matter where it comes from.

Lemme see if this works Gregory thought. *I'll keep my job at Sea World and make a few little transactions on the side and see how easy it goes.* It was too easy. He met a guy from Atlanta who attended Devry University and who tried to persuade him to relocate and enroll. Gregory gave it some thought but ultimately decided the illegal drug industry was his shortcut to wealth and status, but as a cover informed his mother he was moving to Atlanta to go to college. She was excited. Her boy was going to do good.

G rides back toward the familiarity of his Bankhead neighborhood, the beer and pot making him mellow and relaxed. He isn't worried that the deal did not transpire, and if the guy calls him again he will go back. Just because a guy doesn't show for a dinner reservation doesn't mean you turn him away the next time he comes to the restaurant. Whenever he wants to spend money, let him spend it.

The bike and its rider are on Bankhead and the usual smattering of street dwellers take note that G from Miami (although he's not really from Miami) is cruising, and they watch with subtle respect for they wish to protect him and not to highlight his presence. He is important. He holds his head high, always observant, relaxed yet attentive, cool yet wise. He is back on Bankhead when he notices two state troopers parked on a side street, and they seem to take note of him. *Strange* he thinks. *Those dudes don't usually come down here in the 'hood. The highway is usually their turf.* He wonders if they are looking for someone. He wonders if they are looking for him.

It took Gregory about a minute to become an expert in trafficking. It started with a trip to Atlanta with his best friend, Kenny. They hauled five kilos of cocaine across the state line and crossed the flat lands of South Georgia and up to the capitol city. The crystallized form of the party drug was growing in popularity and business was hot. Atlanta was wide open and the newcomers from Florida began to establish themselves as premier crack dealers in the city's poverty-stricken and problem-riddled neighborhoods. The "Miami Boys" were revered by most and feared by some. They carried a mystique about them, like mercenary assassins setting up tents among common soldiers. The people had no idea these young men were brand new at their trade and were themselves masking fear. The crusty, cocky outer shell was necessary, but inside they knew they had chosen a high risk career and that they could momentarily land in prison or in a box.

It isn't like G to panic. He is usually cool as the other side of the pillow but his present condition and circumstances produce uncommon anxiety that borders on paranoia. He is sure he is over the legal limit for alcohol, would certainly test positive for marijuana, and is in possession of twenty-eight grams of cocaine, an amount adequate to warrant a trafficking charge and certain prison time.

The troopers roll out of their positions and onto the street, moving slowly and deliberately in G's direction. The traffic light ahead turns yellow, then red and the bike's rider groans and swallows hard. He has to make a decision, and he has to make it fast.

The long drives to Miami, Daytona and Jacksonville were tedious, but the payoffs were well worth it. Gregory learned the tricks of the trade and was soon piling up enough cash to fill garbage bags. One of the "tricks" was that a drug dealer cannot use his real name. It doesn't take long for word to spread that a new guy in town is filling the streets with bags of dope, and the word always makes its way to the authorities and they begin to put together a profile to find out who the guy is. If they know your name it doesn't take long for them to find you. Atlanta's cops knew about G within days after he arrived, but they did not know he was Gregory Tyrone Washington, a former Sea World employee from Orlando. They only knew him by a letter. His true identity had been reduced to nothing more than an uneventful curved line with a little doo-dad added to distinguish it from the letter C. Alone the letter G represents nothing but itself and makes no particular statement and changes no one's mind about anything. It is merely the seventh letter of the English alphabet and is used less often than eighty percent of the other letters. Linguistically, it can accomplish nothing without the support of other letters. It needs help to become more than a lowly, hump-backed blot. It needs inspiration to become something of meaning and purpose. It needs to experience linguistic evolution.

He sees the troopers again and the decision is made: *I ain't goin' to jail today.* G bends over the bike's handlebars and revs the engine. It sounds like a massive bumblebee as he explodes through the red light, pops a wheelie and streaks down Bankhead with frightening ferocity. By the time he reaches the Hollywood Road split the speedometer is pegged at 130 and the game is over. They will never catch him.

At Hollywood Road, Bankhead bears to the left and continues as a main four lane street out to I 285 and into Mableton. Hollywood bears right and is narrower and less travelled. G makes the decision to take Hollywood. There is less visibility and it is more precarious for the troopers, *if* they are still following. He leans slightly to negotiate the turn but something is wrong. It's as if the handlebars are locked and he can go nowhere but straight ahead. At 130 mph, one covers ground very quickly, and before he can flinch the young man is on the ground with the motorcycle and is sliding across the terrain. The bike and rider had zoomed straight toward a utility pole, but at the last second swerved the slightest bit and avoided sudden impact. Rather, they had barely clipped the pole.

The young man slides to a stop just a few feet from his bike. His mind is now racing in high gear, and although he is amazed he is still alive nothing supersedes the idea that he has to get out of here before law enforcement arrives. He feels a little shaken but jumps to his feet, only to collapse like a jelly statue. Sirens wail. He looks down to discover the awful truth. Where his knee cap should be is a gaping hole. The knee cap is gone.

Gregory was born to run. He was created to glide like a gazelle and make his adversaries look foolish. From the time he was old enough to hold a ball it was in his blood to compete. His sport was the sport that was in season, and his talent combined with leadership qualities resulted in respect by peers and coaches and frequent appointments as team captain. Gregory was an athlete. He had strong shoulders and a solid core. He was quick and savvy. Gregory never thought of the possibility of crippling injuries, debilitating diseases or a premature exit from this world. He carried a subconscious presumption of invincibility, as is common in many young men. After his sophomore year in high school he opted for a job rather than continued involvement with team sports, but still got together with the fellas to keep the skills sharp.

G lies on a gurney in the trauma center and wonders about his future. Will he lose his leg? If not, will he be able to walk normally? Can this type of injury potentially kill him? As if floating on the clouds of a dream he watches a technician walk past carrying a container with his knee cap inside. It was severed from his leg as if blown off by a shotgun. He wonders if doctors can reattach it, wonders what his mother and grandmother will do when they get the news. Suddenly his thoughts are interrupted. Attention turns to a patient on the next table and G is left to wait. Through questions and answers from the doctors and nurses he picks up information about his counterpart, a young black male who is victim of assault with a knife by his girlfriend. His injuries are life-threatening. There is a lot of blood and the team is fighting very hard to control bleeding from several spots. They seem to be losing the battle. The monitor next to the table reveals the usual white line that jumps with each heartbeat to form a mountain range of life. They are beautiful, jagged peaks that let everyone know the human being on the table is still holding on. But momentarily the mountains begin to move further apart and reduce to foothills, then bumps in the road, then a straight highway to the next life. The beeps run together and become a soul-stirring death knell. The team works frenetically for another unfruitful five minutes. The doctor in charge makes his morbid announcement.

O God, please don't let me die. Just give me a chance. I don't want to die.

As to the evolution of *G,* I was not there for the entire event, but I sat with the man that once was *G* and he recounted in great detail the stages of evolution through which he lived. His rhetoric is compelling and emanates a genuineness that belies doubt. Besides, what would motivate this man to lie? He once rode the streets in "pimped out" classic cars, bought and sold houses like I buy candy bars and searched for creative ways to hide bundles of cash. His story contains the themes movies are made of: The foolishness of youth, high speed chases, second chances, crime, violence and horror, a mother's love. He lived according to his own agenda for thirty-two years, made lots of money and had lots of "stuff," but was reduced to a single letter and a series of numbers, his prison identification. The gifts he was born with were buried under piles of fall-out produced by years of rebellion and self-reliance. They were still there, just buried.

From the time the boy was conceived in his mother's womb, Father's plan for Gregory Tyrone Washington never changed. His desire for this precious son never altered. The gifts were still waiting and the promises still real, but disobedience has a way of making our blessings much harder to realize and our purpose much more difficult to see. Self-reliance produces filters in the spiritual eyes, ears and mind, making it intriguing and confusing to associate thoughts and ideas with God. As we develop patterns of choosing our own way over the way God has prepared for us, we slowly pull a blindfold over our spiritual eyes and clog our spiritual ears with the cotton of our own arrogance. The longer we walk our own path the more we pile upon ourselves hindrances to understanding and receiving Father's words and pictures.

Eve and Adam were victims of deception. They were tricked into believing there was a better way than God's way. They became convinced they could run their own lives more effectively than the One who created them. The results of their initial decision were catastrophic, and their lives were immediately filled with obstacles and distractions to all the gifts and blessings sons and daughters are supposed to have. The blessings were still there. They were just much harder to find.

Gregory was victim of the same deception as his most ancient ancestors. From the time of his birth a serpent was assigned to whisper in his ear, and through the vulnerability of youth, convinced him he was strong, powerful and capable of managing his own life. He was told that money was the key to happiness and there was an easy path to gaining wealth and status. As a very young man Gregory decided he could never be anything more than a hustler and drug dealer on the streets of Atlanta. Although the "fruit" came in abundance (money, possessions, women), in a direct parallel to Eve and Adam the young man lost his identity and began to hide and deny his purpose. To reveal who he really was would have resulted in a date with reality and accountability.

Even after God spared his life (one does not crash a motorcycle at 130 miles per hour and live to tell about it), G resolved he could never do anything else and would never call anyone "boss." In fact, he became much more serious about his business and about his commitment to trust his own ways. By his own words he took more of a "no nonsense" approach to selling illegal drugs. G prospered and thrived for the next decade, doing things *his* way, living by *his* wits, putting into practice *his* best ideas. He organized a Limited Liability Company and began to hide his illegal dealings under the umbrella of the business. He used the business to launder piles of cash accumulated through the sale of illegal drugs. After the turn of the century G actually began to think about giving up trafficking and making a living the old fashioned way, but it was still *his* plan, born of his own intellect and void of the Purpose for which Father created him.

In his poem "To a Mouse," Robert Burns pens the following line: "The best laid schemes of mice and men / Go oft awry." Little did G know that his "best laid schemes" could so quickly shatter, especially when his thoughts were turning toward a more honest lifestyle. The formula for G's demise made no sense. In 2002 a house he was buying was busted for drugs, but he did not live there, did not have an outright deed to the property, was not present when the bust took place. He rented the place to a couple of young thugs, and he knew what they were doing but there was no way to prove it. The police searched the house and found nothing, but one officer would not give up, declaring he was sure there was something there and persisting until canine units were brought in to search. Immediately one of the dogs alerted on a door facing and a quick demolition revealed the hiding place for a large stash of cocaine and an automatic pistol. The residents were required to give the landlord's name and G was called to the property.

G was arrested for possession of and trafficking cocaine and possession of a firearm by a convicted felon. He was found guilty and the judge sentenced him to twenty years in state prison for the drug charges, but ignored the gun charge (a mandatory five year sentence in a federal penitentiary) because the judge was anxious to get to a party and it was getting late. "Double jeopardy" would prevent the legal system from revisiting the gun charge. After more than two years in state prison, the original sentence of twenty years was modified to ten, with parole eligibility set at forty months. G did his time like an honor student and made parole on the first review.

Prison was never part of the original equation for the young man from Orlando, but incarceration put him in a place where Yahweh could get his attention. G began to hear Father's words and see His pictures and realized there was a plan bigger than his own. He surrendered his life to Jesus Christ and began to consume the ways and thoughts of Yahweh on a steady basis. He began to study the Word and seek counsel from Father concerning the big and little things in his life. He decided obedience to the instructions he found there was a good idea. He was tired of depending on himself.

Many miracles happened along the way, but the greatest miracle of all is that G died in prison and Gregory Tyrone Washington was reborn. The young man that God created with great gifts, talents and leadership skills was spiritually resurrected in prison and was set back on course to realize his Purpose. While behind prison walls G began to realize all that had been stolen from him and embarked on a journey to find the One who could restore it. He started to regain his identity and Father proceeded to make His purpose clear and to validate Gregory as a true son. By the time he walked out everyone knew him as Greg, the guy who says, "All that stuff I brought into prison, I'm leaving it right here. I ain't takin' nothin' back out with me."

Greg had lost his vision for the street. He was tired of "pickin' that snake up straight by the tail." He had been bitten more than once and was fully aware the next bite could kill him. A new vision was born, one that included discipleship, worship and service. He began to come to City of Refuge to use the workout facility. While in prison Greg had developed the physique of a bodybuilder, but a severe limp still reminds him of Father's mercy. He found out about the feeding ministry City of Refuge operates on the ghetto's street corners and parking lots and began to show up and help serve. On one occasion a homeless man in the feeding line kept staring and finally asked, "G, is that you?" Not sure the man would understand if Greg told him G was dead, he just smiled and nodded. "Wow" the man exclaimed. "If you can change *anybody* can."

A "brother" from Florida heard about the transformation and drove to Atlanta to verify that G from the streets had changed. He came looking for G but found Greg and hardly recognized the man he saw.

2011

A young man navigates his way down Mayson Turner Road, crosses the railroad tracks and turns in to Chappell Forest, a neighborhood notorious for drugs, prostitution and other malevolent behavior. He is driving a white fifteen passenger Ford van and he is on a mission. He has deliveries to make. He sits straight and tall in the driver's seat, very serious about his duties and absolutely committed to his mission. A worship song drifts from the van's speakers and the driver taps the steering wheel in time with the rhythm and hums the melody.

His name is Gregory Tyrone Washington, Youth Pastor at The Mission, A Place of Refuge. The teens in his group call him Pastor Greg. He has evolved from talented athlete, to culinary prospect, to street thug and drug dealer, to state prisoner, to street feeding volunteer, to laborer in the Compassion Atlanta warehouse, to Youth Pastor (otherwise known as father to the fatherless). He still rolls into the Atlanta's worst housing projects and makes deliveries, only now he delivers young people back to their homes from youth services, discipleship classes, camps and outings. Today they have been to a ball game.

"Hey Brandon, you're home, buddy" he calls to a young passenger on the seat behind him. Brandon makes his way to the side door to exit, thanking his Youth Pastor for the day out and asking him about tomorrow's activity. Greg doesn't answer because someone walking from the apartment toward the next building has caught his attention. He studies the young lady and whispers to himself, *Is that who I think it is?*

"Brandon, who is that lady right there?" he asks.

"Oh, that's my momma" the boy answers. A tear rushes to Greg's eye and he drops his head to the steering wheel to hide it. He covers his emotion well and asks Brandon his mother's name. "Nicole" the youngster answers.

In a voice on the verge of cracking and breaking, Greg tells Brandon goodbye, but sits for a moment staring at the front door after it closes. He remembers the door and the people who lived behind it fifteen years ago when he regularly delivered mini-baggies of crack cocaine and took what little money they had for it. He remembers a young girl who would sometimes answer the door and recalls the raspy, demanding voice of her mother calling from the shadows, "Nicole, who is it?"

"It's somebody for you" Nicole would reply.

What have I done? Greg asks himself. The answer quickly comes:

"It's not about what you have done, but what you are doing and will do. There are two paths before you. One leads to the ghetto and the other to the Garden. Trust your own ideas and make your own way and you will one day realize the path leads only to death. Worship at the Tree of Knowledge and you will fight battles that are not yours, and you will ultimately lose.

On the other hand, hear My voice and do what I say and you will experience My Peace, Power, Provision and Protection all the days of your life. Worship at the Tree of Life and you will discover the great purpose for which you were created and will find the strength and courage to respond in obedience to it. My Life is all you need."

Rock Concert

It is a picture of balance, a metaphor for everything sensuous and pure, a poetic symbol of the intended purpose of mankind. It is filled with love, harmony, generosity, cooperation, respect and goodwill. It is a rock concert.

As I stand here with fifty thousand of my closest friends (all but two of whom I have never met), amid the lights and sounds and vibrations, my soul is captivated by the beauty of the experience. There is beauty in harmony. There is beauty in truth. There is beauty in innovation and the simple use of blessed gifts. My soul is stirred by the beauty and I am made to know there is something ecclesiastic about it.

There are nameless brothers and sisters spread out in every direction and climbing giant staircases to rapturous heights, but all leaning in toward the nucleus, the soul of the gathering. He (the soul) occupies a half acre of space in the center, at times focused and intense, at other times wild and chaotic. But, no matter his manner or method, the crowd reacts in euphoric response. I become convinced they will do anything he asks.

Man is created with an urge to worship, an inner compulsion to recognize that which is majestic and bow before it. He must acknowledge the most creative, talented, beautiful and inspirational elements on earth, human and otherwise. Although massive numbers of human beings have never heard of the Scripture verse, deep inside each of us is an innate knowledge that Apostle James was right when he declared, "Every good and perfect gift is from above, coming down from the Father of the heavenly lights" (James 1:17). If it is good, it came from God. Period.

The man on stage wails a soulful lament on the world's injustices and finishes his hymn at the front of the stage, bowed on one knee. Stage lights flash in brilliant colors and the guitar rings out the haunting introduction to the next song. All around me hands are raised to the sky and people sway or bounce to the rhythm. The drummer and bassist join the melody and rise from a low, steady beat, like a fighter jet approaching the top of the runway, slowly increasing speed and intensity until the song takes off with a deafening roar and an indescribable surge of energy, taking fifty thousand ecstatic passengers with it.

But, as the bass pounds in my chest and I sing along with the familiar lyric, "I want to run, I want to hide, I want to tear down the walls that hold me inside," my eyes are drawn to the people around me and I am struck by what I see. I continue to sing but am now focused on my brothers and sisters, people who are ordinary like me, people who work jobs, go to school, raise families and pay taxes. Most of them are singing as well, "I want to reach out and touch the flame, where the streets have no name," but many of them are doing other things also. For them the music alone is not good enough. The fellowship of this great community is insufficient to satisfy. They must add something to the gift. They must create ways to make colors brighter, experiences more memorable and sounds more poignant. I notice hundreds of liquor and beer bottles on the ground and at least a third of the people are working to add to the number. As we sing, "I want to feel sunlight on my face, I see the dust cloud disappear without a trace," the guy behind me applies fire to a bong and immediately a wave of marijuana smoke wafts across my face. I resist the urge to inhale deeply (in case I run for President some day), and instead fan the smoke away and cough dramatically. People look at me like I'm weird.

"I want to take shelter from the poison rain, where the streets have no name." The stage has mobile bridges on each side that stretch to a circular runway extending into the audience, and as we sing with passion and urgency the bridge on my side begins to move and stops just above my head. I am watching a middle-aged lady extract a half-pint of whiskey from her boot and pour it into a half empty Pepsi bottle, when I notice people pointing above. The crescendo has escalated as some scream and others continue to sing, "The city's aflood and our love turns to rust, we're beaten and blown by the wind, trampled in dust," and I look up to see the singer on the bridge with his leg thrown over the rail as if he is going to drop to the floor and join us. He holds out the microphone and the people sing louder, "I'll show you a place high on a desert plain, where the streets have no name." He leans over the rail and drops of sweat fall onto those of us directly below him. Ladies squeal like little girls on Christmas morning and grown men stare at the gleaming sweat spots as if gold nuggets just rained from the heavens.

The next gust of pot smoke catches me off guard and I really do choke, causing the inebriated guy next to me to pat my shoulder and through a half-cocked grin inquire, "You alright bro?" He is genuinely interested in my well-being, proven next by his offer of "a shot of the hair of the dog?" He produces a pint bottle of Jim Beam and extends it my way, expecting me to put my lips where his lips have been. That's what drunks do.

"No thanks" I reply. "I have some water."

Our Father gives good gifts. It has always been so and will remain as an undeniable truth for all of eternity. In Genesis 2 the Father knelt in the dirt and formed man in His own image, giving man His own breath, the first of an inexhaustible list of good gifts. Immediately, the Father desired to bless His son with an unsoiled place to live.

"And the Lord God planted a garden eastward in Eden; and there He put the man whom He had formed" (Genesis 2:8).

Man was not made for the garden; the garden was made for man. In addition, everything in the garden was made for man. Trees, plants, pure water, animals, Peace, tranquility, shelter from outside dangers, perfect provision, good health, and the list goes on and on. But when man disobeyed and ate of the fruit of the Tree of Knowledge of Good and Evil, he forfeited automatic access to every "good and perfect gift" and now spends his days trying to retrieve what was lost. He is chasing a feeling, the feeling of belonging to a family and having some purpose for living. He is searching for a shade tree that he can lean against and find protection from the brutal sun, or a warm refuge where he can take shelter from the wind and rain. He is reaching here and there, grasping and grappling for provision and answers. His mind is a whirlwind of questions and retorts that do not align with each other. His life is like a race car that has crashed and flipped upside down, and the driver still has the accelerator pressed to the floor but the wheels only spin in sad, fruitless revolutions. Within the spirit of man is a giant rupture into which he continually crams debris that he collects along life's road. But with each deposit of garbage, the feeling of emptiness only grows. The rupture is shaped like God, and only He can fill it completely.

Worship is a simple thing. It is to act in a manner that acknowledges our Creator and the good gifts He has afforded us. It is to recognize that we have nothing without Him and that our best efforts, if not linked to His plan, are only spinning wheels on a life that is upside down. Worship is to live in a manner that reflects His image, whether in church, at home or at a rock concert. If a professional athlete acknowledges his ability to perform on the field as a blessed gift from his Creator, and that he could perform no better than a helpless infant without the gift, then every stride, hit, catch, kick, move and breath is a praise unto his Father. On the other hand, one who counts his success solely as a result of his own hard work and personal prowess worships only himself.

Hard work is admirable, but we must remember that the ability to work hard is a gift from God. Intelligence is something to be applauded, but failure to acknowledge that every positive intellectual thought has its origin in Yahweh's omniscience is to discount His gift and credit ourselves with divine work. Every good and perfect gift originates in the heart of the Father. What we do with it after He gives it to us bears great accountability.

A few years ago I was enjoying another concert, this one in Atlanta's Piedmont Park. One of America's most popular music groups was performing. They drew a crowd of more than fifty thousand as well and featured one of the greatest drummers to ever pick up a pair of sticks. As I stood on the grass on a pleasant September evening, listening to good music and contemplating the irony of a "green concert" in a park littered with several tons of garbage, I was amazed at the things the drummer could do behind the kit. The speed, agility, timing and coordination required to play the rhythms defied human capabilities. At one point the guy next to me yelled out, "Man, have you ever seen a dude work the drums like that?"

"He has a natural gift" I replied, but I knew the answer was wrong as soon as I spoke. Fact is the drummer's gift is not natural; rather, it is supernatural. When I witnessed the phenomenal execution of musical aptitude, I witnessed the handiwork of the Father, as much as the massive oak trees that outline the park declared the same. The glory of the night sky was no more a testimony to the creative omnipotence of Yahweh than was the ability of the guitarist to paint brilliant sound colors on his strings. The flowers and streams testified to His majesty, but so did the raspy voice of the band's vocalist.

Man is very proud of himself and spends untold hours and billions of dollars recognizing himself for what he has done. He rolls out the red carpet for those who are especially gifted and calls to the stage those who have performed exceptionally. He plasters the faces and bodies of the world's sexiest and most gorgeous people on the covers of magazines and on the television screen, applauding himself for being beautiful, successful and creative. Upon his exodus from the Garden, man assumed charge of his existence on earth and continues to chase fulfillment and to lavish upon himself glory and praise for his great accomplishments. But man never finds ultimate satisfaction in his feats or in the resulting rewards and awards. He still chases his own ideas and creates new accolades to reward his perceived greatness. Man is praised for "reinventing" himself when he demonstrates the ability to adjust to changing times and trends.

In other words, rather than submitting himself in humble worship and service to his Creator, man continues to compete with God and to make decisions for self-sufficiency. In that sense not much has changed since Eve and Adam believed the serpent's lie. Man still believes more knowledge will elevate him to divine status. He still worships and depends on his own ideas and goes to great lengths to celebrate his own accomplishments. He sets up flashy and beautiful spiritual facades and spends his days worshipping his creation, but the foundation is a sand pile that will not hold when the storm arises. Man is on a mission to build a kingdom that will afford him everything that satisfies and brings fulfillment to his life. Yes, the thing for which mankind searches is *fulfillment.* I want to have enough money to have and do whatever I want. I want my relationships to be satisfying and problem-free. I want to be in perfect health and never have to suffer or feel the effects of growing old. I long for knowledge that will present me with answers to great mysteries and solutions to magnificent problems. I want to be fulfilled.

Although knowledge, talent, creativity and strength are gifts from God, and as such bear no unfavorable intent toward those who receive them, so often we strive in a manner that is outside the will and purpose of the Father to use these gifts in selfish pursuits. We do not seek His counsel or walk in a pattern of obedience that will insure results in line with His intentions. We take the main ingredients to His recipe for fulfillment and begin to add our own flavors and seasonings. By our actions we declare that His ideas are not quite good enough, so we help Him along, obeying our intuitions rather than His word. The result is usually something that satisfies for a moment, but leaves us to start over after the first stiff wind.

My mother makes the best coconut pie in the world. As we say around my house, "It's documented." A couple years ago I decided to begin a new tradition and cook dinner for the family on Mother's Day. For dessert, I chose to make my mother's coconut pie. For days prior to the big event I anxiously anticipated the opportunity to showcase my culinary skills - sweet and sour chicken with fresh pineapples and bell peppers, fried rice, mixed vegetables, and hot, buttery dinner rolls. But mostly, I looked forward to presentation of a fabulous coconut pie with flaky crust filled to the brim with creamy, coconutty goodness, and topped with fluffy meringue, barely browned and capped with toasted coconut flecks. It would be the highlight of a marvelous meal.

Mom gladly provided the recipe for the pie, a trusted and revered recipe that for decades held hallowed esteem. It was presented on an index card and written in my mother's own handwriting, adding even more to the authenticity and excitement of the experience. I made the pie first so it could "set and cool" and never doubted Mom's instruction to "Enjoy!" I couldn't wait for my wife, her mother, and our friend, Brenda, to fork a yummy hunk of that pie into their mouths and declare with coconut flecks hanging from their lips that I had once again proven my value to the human race. The anticipation was incredible.

Everyone seemed to enjoy the chicken, rice, vegetables and rolls. They said they never knew I could cook like that and that we needed to "do this more often." In the back of my mind I was thinking, *you ain't seen nothing yet!* I cleared the table, got out the dessert dishes, and placed a beautiful wedge of that glorious pie onto each one. As I served them, the ladies oohhed and aahhed, and I proudly announced, "It's my mother's recipe."

My mother-in-law, Faye, was the first to sample the pie, and I instantly discerned something was wrong. She commented that the pie was "good" but her body language suggested something altogether different. Her second bite was significantly smaller than the first and it seemed to me that she swallowed very quickly. O well, I thought, it will take a few bites for something this good to fully manifest itself. One can't possibly pass judgment on a mere couple of bites. I poured Brenda more tea as Faye continued to nibble like a mouse on a block of cheddar, and my wife, Tracy, began to perceive by her mother's demeanor that something was not quite right and to look questioningly at me.

Now, there are two things one can count on from Brenda: 1. She will never refuse dessert. 2. She will be brutally honest. I placed the dish in front of her and waited for her grand exclamation that this was the best coconut pie she had ever eaten and that she could not believe the extent of my talents in the kitchen. Instead, she took one bite and began to gag and sputter, grabbing her napkin and discharging every speck of the pie into it, even swabbing her tongue in an effort to rid herself of the flavor. She coughed dramatically and gulped her tea, and when finally able to speak demanded boisterously, "IS THIS A JOKE?!"

I learned that day the importance of following the recipe to the letter and accepting no substitutes. As an inexperienced pie maker, I had no idea that pure vanilla is much different than vanilla flavoring, and that too much pure vanilla will take your breath. I also learned how important it is to do more than just read the words and make modifications where one sees fit. I was ready to be the world's best pie maker, yet I had never gone over the recipe with Mom to make sure I understood it. I had never stood by her side and taken note of the brand names used, watched as she measured and stirred, listened as she elaborated on each step in the process, asked questions along the way. I could read the words on the card but really did not understand my mother's heart for this pie. I stood at the head of my dining room table, arrogantly awaiting proclamations on my success, only to hear Brenda proclaim brashly, "That's the worst thing I've ever put in my mouth. It tastes like my colonoscopy medicine." My best effort to produce something satisfying and memorable was tossed face down into the garbage can.

God's gifts are good enough, and if I stand near to Him, He will show them to me and teach me how to use them. If I am careful to employ the gifts and talents He has placed in me, within the context of His will and purpose for my life, I will experience great satisfaction and fulfillment, and others will be blessed as well. As I stand under the stars and the music runs through my soul, I see people trying to worship, but they have modified the recipe and added lots of things that don't belong. Many have never considered that Yahweh has an individual plan for them, a recipe for life, and massive numbers of others who believe He made them and loves them have never sat with the Father and allowed Him to elaborate on the words they have heard and read. They only know Him as a distant deity, but have never stood near enough to hear His instructions and understand His heart.

The singer has moved to the far side of the stage and is giving the patrons on that side an equal chance to take home a drop of sweat. The guitar is ringing out the intro to a song off the new album, and the crowd reacts with ecstatic enthusiasm. It feels like the first drop on a massive roller coaster, and I wonder if the whole place may momentarily combust.

He runs to the front of the loop which extends far into the audience and reaches the point just as the band evens out the melody to allow the first line, "I was born, I was born to be with you in this space and time." Sons and daughters of Yahweh sing with him, but I think few have any idea what they are really saying. "After that, and ever after, I haven't had a clue. Only to break rhyme, this foolishness can leave a heart black and blue." I wasn't with the songwriter when he penned these words, and he has never given me a personal explanation, so I will not be so presumptuous as to declare their meaning, but the beauty of art is that it can mean different things to different people. At the moment, this stadium is a house of satire for me, a place where so many elements of worship exist, and man's potential is reflected in so many ways, but where there is little understanding of why we are on this planet "in this space and time." We have ruptured the continuity between our Father, ourselves, and the rest of creation, and the "rhyme" the Father intended has become muddled and unrecognizable. The harmony, peace, and satisfaction have been broken, leaving us writing an awful lyric on the human condition. As the song proclaims, "...this foolishness can leave a heart black and blue."

Brothers and sisters lift their hands, sway their bodies, and close their eyes, and I believe they do so with worship as their hidden, undetected motivation. But their hearts are "black and blue." They have been "beaten and blown by the wind" and have not turned to their Maker for help. They have looked to music, drugs, alcohol, sex, food, money, therapy, possessions, beauty, and a million other things, when what they need is God. The singer wails, "I was born, I was born to sing for you, I didn't have a choice but to lift you up and sing whatever song you wanted me to." He lifts his head to view the night sky, his right hand reaching upward in a grasping motion, rocking up and down on the balls of his feet and extending the fingertips as far as possible, as if the desired object is just out of reach. "I give you back my voice, from the womb, my first cry, it was a joyful noise."

The Father created us intentionally and with great purpose in mind. It is His chief desire that we maintain closeness with Him so He may reveal this great purpose and give consistent instruction on how we should manage it. He has things to tell and pictures to reveal. Real worship happens when we begin to hear His words and see His pictures and respond in obedience to what we hear and see. His glory is revealed and we begin to understand the words we sing and the motivations behind our actions. Everything becomes justified, reconciled into perfect balance, and we come to understand we do not need the things the world offers. We do not need fleeting forms of false contentment. We simply need Him. As the singer declares in the last refrain, "Justified till we die, you and I will magnify, Oh, the Magnificent."

Only God can fill a God-shaped hole.

Quotations from U2 songs:
"Where the Streets Have No Name"
"Magnificent"

WHAT WOULD JESUS DO?!

The following constitutes the biography of a human being created by the God of the universe, conceived and born in customary fashion some 40 or 45 years ago.

- His name was Dennis Lamar Thomas

- He was tall, skinny and black, with an oversized Adam's apple

- He smelled bad

- He wore "high water" pants

- He was a homeless crack addict and alcoholic for more than 10 years

- He died of complications from AIDS

- He was buried in a pauper's grave (I don't know exactly where)

I suppose I could write "The End" here and move on to the next story. I think, however, it's appropriate to give some attention to Dennis in his death, as there is so little to note from his life.

First of all, I must confess that sometimes Dennis got on the nerve right next to my last one. He always wanted something (not a new concept in urban ministry). Dennis' running list of requests included food, clean socks, shoes without holes, a prescription filled, a ride to the crack dealer, oops, I mean the "auto shop." Dennis loved to exercise obedience to the Scripture, "Ask and you shall receive...", and I don't recall him ever offering to give back. There was no limit to the asking. In typical fashion, he would disappear at times for several days or even weeks, but when Dennis was around he always had his hand out.

Somewhere along the line someone with a significant level of numbness between the ears introduced Dennis to the catchy Christian question, "What would Jesus do?"

"Dennis, I don't have time to take you to Northside. I'm late already."

"But, Pastor, what would Jesus do?"

"Dennis, there's no food in the kitchen and I am short on cash."

"But, Pastor, I'm hungry. What would Jesus do?"

"Dennis, you can't ride in my car any more. The last time you rode with me you left a stain on the passenger seat."

"But, Pastor, my feet have blisters and I can barely walk. What would Jesus do?"

"What would Jesus do?" I'd like to find the person who introduced Dennis to that concept and do something Jesus wouldn't do, like maybe pop them with a taser a few times to get the mental log jams cleared up. I'm sorry, but the question frustrates me. I am sure it was not the intention of the slogan's creator, but the result is, nonetheless, frustration. Although the thinking behind the question is pretty obvious, am I really to take it literally? To answer that question, we must, as a measuring stick for what Jesus would do, take a look at some of the things he actually did. Here are a few examples:

1. He healed people instantly. In ancient times lepers were the social equivalent of modern day AIDS victims. They were "untouchable" and people were afraid of them. Jesus simply looked at them and said, "Be clean," and they were. One minute they had spots; the next minute they didn't. One minute their bodies were racked with disease; the next minute they were given a clean bill of health. One minute they were social outcasts; the next minute they were back in their homes, churches and marketplaces. That's what Jesus did; I can only assume that's what He *would do* (see Luke 17:11-14).

2. Jesus blessed and broke tiny portions of food and multiplied it to feed thousands of people. He didn't have to spend money. He didn't have to drive to Sam's and stand in the checkout line. He didn't have to cook, and He even made someone else clean up. He just blessed it, broke it and gave it away, and it just kept coming, even after all bellies were full. The Gospels tell us that the disciples collected basketfuls of leftovers. I sometimes wonder if, somewhere in the Holy Land, someone is still eating that bread and fish. After all, Jesus blessed it. At any rate, that's what Jesus did, so I can only assume that's what He *would do* (see Mark 6:30-44).

3. Jesus exercised authority over nature. On one occasion He stood on the deck of a boat during a violent storm and commanded the storm, "Be still." The winds were instantly quieted, and the waves sat down. Another time He came to the disciples as they sailed, walking casually on top of the water. He didn't have to rent a paddle boat or a jet ski; He just strolled. That's what Jesus did; I can only assume that's what He *would do* (see Mark 4:35-41; 6:45-50).

4. Jesus spoke and dead carcasses were reunited with their souls and lived again. Wow, He raised the dead! This caps it all. On the occasion of the death of His friend, Lazarus, Jesus responded to the call of Mary and Martha, but He arrived too late to prevent Lazarus' passing. Their beloved brother had been gone for four days, and by his own sister's account, his body had started to become (in ghetto lingo) "musty." Jesus said a simple prayer and told His friend to come out of the tomb. In an instant, the once-dead Lazarus walked out in his grave clothes. "What would Jesus do?" I can only assume that what He *did* is what He *would do* (see John 11).

Can you identify with my frustration? It is a feeling that is affirmed and justified by one simple fact: I CAN'T DO WHAT JESUS DID! It is a more unreasonable challenge than to ask me to do what Masters champion Phil Mickelson would do at the sixteenth hole at Augusta National. Neither my desire to do it...nor my acquisition of expensive equipment...nor my less-than-illustrious swing will bring about the desired result. Playing golf and going to the beach are similar experiences for me – plenty of sand and water. Please don't ask me to do what Phil would do. The inevitability of failure would produce stress and frustration, making the situation worse rather than better.

Likewise, please don't ask me to do what Jesus would do because, as badly as I would like to, I can't do what He would do. What would Jesus have done for Dennis? Based on the documented precedent, He would likely say, "Be clean" and would subsequently instruct Dennis to go tell his pastor his AIDS was gone. Jesus would most certainly have made miraculous provision for Dennis' nutritional needs. Maybe the Savior would have touched the worn, smelly sneakers Dennis wore and they would have become brand-new Reeboks in an instant. Jesus would have, with a word, delivered Dennis from the demons of alcoholism and drug addiction and given him a long, healthy life. He might have called Dennis to follow Him and become part of His inner circle of friends, passing on to him the keys to the Kingdom and revealing secrets straight from the heart of the Father.

Can you see the dilemma? Can you feel the frustration? Have you, perhaps, been frustrated that you cannot live up to the Utopian standard the church has presented as discipleship? While the question "What would Jesus do?" rattles around in the far reaches of my brain, the lifeless body of Dennis Lamar Thomas rots in an unmarked, overgrown grave somewhere in Atlanta. Why? Because I could not *do* what Jesus *would do.*

Perhaps there is a fairer question we should ask ourselves. I doubt if it will become the theme for a song or will ever adorn shirts and bracelets, but it is, nonetheless, a fairer question. Are you ready? Here it is: What should *I* do?

It is a simple question with a simple answer – OBEY! When the day is done, whether I responded in humble obedience to Father's instruction concerning my own will and purpose is all that will matter. He sent Jesus to earth to accomplish a very specific task. Jesus made it clear that He understood the orders and was willing to walk in strict obedience to the voice that issued them. On many occasions He declared that He came to accomplish the will of the Father. Not only was Jesus' obedience paramount to the success of Father's plan, but He also gave instructions to His followers and expected absolute obedience from them (John 6:38-40; Matthew 7:21; see also Romans 12: 1, 2).

What should *I* do? I should do what He tells me to do. Many believers are frustrated that they cannot hear the voice of God and therefore do not know what to do or how to do it. Fact is, it takes practice to be able to hear the voice of God, and if we are not living in obedience to the commands of Scripture that apply to us all, how can we expect God to trust us with new things? The regular practice of obedience to clear and inarguable instructions found in Scripture will put us in proper position and will open our ears to be able to hear new instruction relative to our purpose, and the courage to respond in obedience. Just as Father sent Jesus to earth to accomplish a specific task, so He has sent each of us to do His will as it has already been spoken in the heavens (see Matthew 6:10).

If we are to do exactly what Jesus did, why has He not empowered us that way? How many dead people have you raised? How many ponds have you strolled on? Do your Cheerios eventually run out, or are they endless like the bread and fish?

If you are struggling to know what to do, begin by responding in humble obedience to the things we have all been charged to do:

- Bring the children to Jesus for the Kingdom is full of them (see Matthew 19:13-15)

- Love the Lord with all your heart, mind, soul and strength, and love your neighbor as you love yourself. By the way, Jesus' story indicates that "neighbor" crosses all barriers – race, background, age, social class and religious affiliation (see Luke 10:25-37).

- Feed the hungry, give water to the thirsty, clothe the naked, visit the prisoners, and be a friend to the lonely. Feed His sheep and lambs (see Matthew 25:31-46; John 21:15-17).

- Take good care of widows and orphans (see Deuteronomy 10:18; Psalm 146; James 1:27).

At the risk of over-simplifying our spirituality, which will inevitably drive the theologians crazy, I guarantee that if you begin to do these things, by the Spirit and in humility, you will begin to grow in understanding of your purpose and will begin to hear the voice of the Father in many forms as He reveals secrets to you and gives you new orders.

Though Dennis often used that dreaded question as ammunition, I walk free of guilt that I did not do what Jesus would do for him; rather, I did what *I* should do, and will do for every Dennis that crosses my path: I fed him, gave him clean clothes and shoes, transported him in my car, helped him get his medicine and cash his check. I wish I could have done what Jesus would have, but I could only do what Father instructed and empowered me to do.

After all, I think that's all Dennis really wanted anyway.

Inspiration, Revelation, Poetry and Prayer

I have a premonition about the upcoming run. As I lace my shoes and go through the pre-run ritual (adjusting my shorts numerous times, applying *Body Glide* to my inner thighs and other parts that tend to chafe, stretching the hip flexers, bouncing to make sure shoe laces do not tick my leg), I have a strong urge that this morning's run will submit and do as I say. I believe it will reflect my extraordinary discipline and afford me six relatively effortless miles rather than four or five lung burners. I believe my forty-nine year old muscles and joints will re-live their twenties and supernaturally revitalize themselves with each step. Surely the third mile will be easier than the second, the fourth easier than the third, and so on. I imagine I will be inspired to write classic poetry and will one day be listed with Frost, Poe and Dickinson in the annals of great American lyricists. After all, I did write the following masterpiece following a smelly run on a swampy nature trail:

Bayou Mystery
I never seen the sun-sung bayou
But I smelt it on the early dawn
Oatmeal, salt tongue, black locke cryin'
Bobtail risin' steady on
Grandmaw sweats 'til none can whisper
Secrets to a banjo dirge
Carved from black trunk towers fallin'
Hammered to the preacher's word
Wrong-eyed outlaws, pilgrims ploddin'
Quick as water on a pond
Death to every sound be lyin'
Death to father, death to son
Black boot, black night on the bayou
Thicker than the goatherd's wool
Lost when lost beyond reprisal
Feeding firelight for the fool
Stay the promise, stay the beauty
Stay the sunlight for a while
Pose the prospect to the mothers
Pass the gate key to the child

If that doesn't rank up there with "The Raven" and "Birches," I don't know what does. I often wonder if Miss Dickinson wrote "A Narrow Fellow in the

Grass" after a stiff five mile jaunt through the countryside surrounding Amherst, Mass. Perhaps she ran past a little black snake, and there you go, classic poetry.

Yes, I believe today's run will be brisk and rewarding. The lungs will prove their conditioning and the legs will belie their years. I will sweat out the body's impurities and will finish as internally clean as the engine of a new car. I will leave two pounds of unwanted girth lying on the road of my personal victory and will finish strong, acknowledging that two more miles would be no problem, if only I had the time.

And the inspiration, oh yes, the inspiration and the resulting classic poetry, like this one about my youngest child, born six days before my forty-first birthday. I wrote it after running and realizing how very tired I was:

Interruption of My Mid-life Crisis
My mid-life crisis was interrupted by bouncing Tiggers and silly old bears
Bats and balls and crayola walls and smelling salts in chestnut hair
Fire trucks running and piggies drum drumming and race cars revving my creaky old bones
Bulldozers dozing and yard hoses hosing and sprinkled vanilla dripping from cones
My slippery slope was candy-coated by sweetness oozing from chocolate drop eyes
Spaghetti eyelashes and Kool-Aid mustaches and potty breaks measuring my patience for size
Bathtub bonanzas and extravaganzas with bubbles and bobbling ships
Bring arthritic glory to my aging story and scurries my worries with words from his lips
My one foot in was snatched quickly out for two is a minimum tumble
Knuckle meals and heads over heels and tension condemned for the sake of the rumble
My autumn reprieve was sentenced to life by life that was sentenced to me
The missing portion, perfectly patterned
A proxy to fountains of sparkling showers and mountains of leaves I can once again see
For Riley – sent like holy breath September 6, 2002

It is the first day of September and the temperature has finally dropped into the upper 60s, a welcome relief after a summer I can only qualify as a distant cousin of hell. It seems the humidity has surrendered its merciless torture and the air is no longer heavy as a dump truck. I'm going to *kill it* this morning. Perhaps I will even formulate an ode to September that can match the following dedication to a glorious November a few years back:

November
Gray light makes grayer shadows
Foretelling autumn's twilight, winter's labor pain
The sky a blue-gray tug-o-war
Like Rebs and Yanks in a trench
A struggle spawning chill wind
Spitting one brown leaf
Falling, calling for reinforcements
Now quickly becoming five hundred, now a thousand
Now sprouting wings like black fighters on nature's mission
Flying for warm lands and green trees
Now growing muscle, bone and sinew
Now twelve becoming one
A honking V splitting the wind like the red man's arrow
Pointing toward some deleterious destination
Some stolid reservation
Some gross miscalculation
Some misinterpretation
Some turbulent frustration
For once it ends, again it begins

I think Carl Sandburg would be proud.

For me there is an intricate connection between running, writing and spirituality. As I start out this morning, I sense the Father wants to give me some of His words and pictures. I feel good and I can't help but think of Adam after he was first created, what a powerful and perfect man he was, and how every breath he inhaled was the unpolluted breath of God, and how there was no excessive heat or humidity with which to contend. As I picture Adam running laps around a fabulous Garden meadow, suddenly I realize I am running like Adam would have run, and I am not yet a half mile in. I am taking long, powerful strides and pumping my arms in rhythm, really legging it out. Maybe today will be the day I will enter that euphoric state of being all runners dream of but almost none achieve, a superhuman, Adamic realm of existence called "the third wind."

Perhaps I will cross over the line that separates casual joggers, who do it because they are out of shape or have high blood pressure, the ones whose doctors have tenderly suggested, "Exercise or die," from serious runners who look like they are sculpted from granite, and who take subscriptions to *Runner's World* and actually read the articles instead of merely looking at the pictures of sleek, sweaty women in tight shorts and sports bras, while munching on a sack of cheese puffs.

I finish the first lap at the county recreation complex, one-half mile on a smooth asphalt track that encircles the soccer practice fields, and I am already starting to feel a little less like pre-fall Adam and a little more like forty-nine year old average Joe who has been victimized by Adam's fruit fest. With every stride my right shoe lace is ticking my ankle, so I cruise to a stop as I come out of the turn and kneel to make an adjustment. I stand again and resume the pace, frustrated that I had to bend over because every ounce of energy counts and every extra motion saps precious drops of it. Funny how four minutes ago I was anticipating "effortless miles" and now I am hoping against hope that I will somehow find the strength to finish, and I am only one lap in. I am paying attention to things like clenched fists, sweat wiping and interrupting breaths to spit wads of cotton. All these things require a little extra energy that I know I will need later.

A black bird has been squawking at me for the past two minutes and I would shoot him if I had my shotgun, but I try not to bring the shotgun to the recreation fields. He is disturbing the peace and… but wait a minute… no…that's poetry!

The Bird
Screech, caw caw caw the black bird squalled
Come rise with me to your God's face
Come soar from this encumb'red place
Screech caw caw caw he bitter swore
Those with the wind need nothing more
He swooped and dove, his challenge clear
His re-ascent sucked up my fear
My heart reached up, my feet bore strong
Poets with wings cannot be wrong
But damn'ed wings they never came
My tethered gait remained the same

With heel and toe hitched to the soil
Fair lungs enraged 'twas such the toil
Then Purpose screamed inside my ear
His voice a trumpet sounding clear
My lips he used his creed to send
To all who chase that wing'd friend
It is to walk walk walk o'er crest and field
Through valley dark and cave concealed
It is to walk walk walk on sandy coast
Down boulevard with human host
It is to run run run through choking dust
'Midst hellish heat and icy gust
It is to run run run in meadow sweet
While black birds in the heavens meet
For earth is home and brothers bear
While squawking foul take to the air
My soul dare not by its disgrace
Leave lone its brothers in this place

Yes, when we give Him a chance, and when we desire them, Father shares very important words and pictures. For me, the solitude and sacrifice of running seem to open the doors of my heart and mind, and in those moments He teaches me powerful things. One lovely spring morning I was into the third mile when I was compelled to pray for a friend of mine. The prayer was like the run, productive and passionate, and as I began to call my friend's name and the names of his wife and children, and to ask the Father to do very specific, significant and extraordinary things in their lives, I began to sense that this prayer was different, special, monumental. I sensed a very real spiritual connection to the Father, and I found myself wanting to go even deeper. I thought of many people and their struggles, brokenness and disappointments, and revelation began to blow over me like a great wind. It was then I realized the prayer was not just for my friend and his family, but the prayer is for many who will read this book, for contained in the pages of this document is woven a prayer of Truth that can set men free. It is a prayer spoken by one man for many. Of the persons for whom I am praying, there are a few I know and multitudes I do not know. The important thing is that the prayer was prayed, and is being prayed, for it is a perpetual offering. The prayer is alive. It breathes and challenges and changes. It calls out, judges and holds accountable. It encourages, heals and applauds. It is a prayer that, if embraced, will lift you out of lion's dens and life flight you out of fiery furnaces. It will give you the courage to take your Savior by the hand and step onto the deck of the battered vessel of your life and pronounce His Peace over the storm that has beaten on you for years. Do you feel yourself wanting to cry? Is there a lump in your throat or a knot in your chest? If so, it is because the Father knows where you are and He knows all the intimate details of your situation. He is going to use this prayer as a powerful spiritual tool to turn your graveyard into a Garden. It is going to happen because this prayer is for you! The Father is making you aware of His great love and compassion toward you, and reminding you, through this word, that He created a Garden for you, and that you can live in the Garden right now.

When I was a kid, people who were bound with all sorts of spiritual chains would come into our church, walk to the front and fall on their faces before God, the preacher and the congregation. They would cry out for forgiveness and the saints would pray with fervor. Some would weep and some would moan, but eventually a shout of joy would arise from the middle of the commotion. I have seen the same people, sober and clear-minded, rise to their feet and begin to weep and worship as if they had just witnessed the ascension firsthand. Tears flowed as individuals ran from their spiritual prisons and were free for the first time in many years. As a youngster, I am sure I did not really connect the prayers to the end result, but I now understand that the prayers had everything to do with it. The prayers of the saints were fervent and relentless, and obedience to the commands of Christ was a way of life. He commanded that we should "ask, seek and knock" (see Matthew 7:7), and the simple, country church-goers took the instruction literally. They simply continued to go back and "ask, seek and knock" over and over and over. Not only were they making prayer requests and praying in church, but there were little old ladies and other "prayer warriors" hammering on Heaven's doors in the solitude of their own bedrooms and closets. There was no hesitation to share the needs and no shyness about calling for an answer. Churches held "prayer meetings" that went for hours (believe me, I slept through many of them), and the brethren would leave exhausted and soaked in sweat. Whether the needy knew it or not, Godly people were calling out their names and agreeing on the same thing, that God would hear them and answer according to His will and purpose.

I want you to know that someone is praying for you! Someone is crying out fervently and the spirit of the exhortation is recorded in this book so that you will always be able to access it. It matters not that we have never met. This is *your* prayer, and you should never doubt it. Through this prayer the power of Almighty God is going to be released to once again miraculously deliver individuals who are bound by addiction and substance abuse, and to teach them that the pathway of obedience leads to Peace, Power, Provision and Protection. I have heard your chains rattle and fall. This prayer will shed a great light in the shadows of deception and will reveal to you how you have been deceived and misled. I have heard the blacksmith's hammer, and I have witnessed the re-designing of your chains. This prayer will escort you into the Garden in which you were intended to live from the beginning, saying farewell forever to the graveyards and ghettos of your past, present and future. I have heard the wind blow.

In the days and weeks following the morning of my magnificent run, the wind of revelation continued to blow. The only challenge to recording all I was seeing and hearing was to find time. The words poured out like water from an open hydrant. There was no digging for ideas, no quest for inspiration, only the fear that something important would fall victim to my wavering memory before I had a chance to write it down. The prayer had to remain alive, both during and between runs, so the Father could continue to reveal His words and pictures.

One particularly humid morning I was struggling through a four-miler at a crisp pace. I was soaked in sweat and was beginning to feel a cramp in the right calf muscle. A hot debate was going on in my mind: Quit and use the cramp as an excuse, or finish out the run while whispering *there are no quitters* in time with every other step. I decided to finish. Just as the decision was made, a cool breeze stirred in the trees, catching me off guard with its freshness and clarity. It defied the day and instantly I knew the Father had something to show me. The wind blew through my eyes like they were opened windows and I saw a giant oak tree, leafy and beautiful, but from its branches hung rotting corpses that swung in the wind, stiff and discolored. Crows lit on them and picked flesh from the ears and eye sockets. As I watched, the knowledge came to me that these were the carcasses of people who had, like Eve, Adam and the young man in my dream, been tricked by the voice of the deceiver. Day after day they had given audience to whispering serpents and had considered their propositions. They had listened to the wrong voices.

The tree was stately and majestic. How could it be worse than any other tree? As I watched, a man approached the tree and knelt quietly at the base of its trunk. I knew he wanted the world's knowledge; he wanted to rule his own life. Another man came and knelt beside him, head bowed. I knew he worshipped the tree rather than the Creator. Suddenly two nooses, deftly hidden behind the beautiful leaves, dropped around the necks of the two men and instantly tightened as some unseen force snatched them and hoisted the captives into the air. For a few moments their bodies thrashed violently, and finally went limp. Immediately, the parasitic birds alighted and began the disgusting task of ripping away the eyes (vision) and mangling the ears (hearing) of the hanging men. Serpents watched whimsically.

The wind blew through nearby trees, and the effect was the most captivating and melodious music I had ever heard. The lyrics were full of truth and life, but the men hanging from the first tree could not see or hear because their eyes and ears were being stripped away and their hearts were rotten unto death.

As the wind continued to blow, my vision was magnified and I began to see possibilities. I saw brilliant, hope-filled possibilities. The first man, the one who first knelt at the foot of the great oak, could awaken from his death sleep. He could raise his hands and head and look above the highest branch, far above his best idea, and could see and touch the One who made him, the One in whose image he was fashioned. IT WAS NOT TOO LATE! He was very, very dead, but he *could* live again! He reeked of pride and smacked of self-gratification, but in an instant he could embrace the life winds that were blowing all around and be re-created, whole and free. It was his possibility – it had his name written on it. As well, I understood it is YOUR possibility. You cannot be *too* dead. There is no such thing as *unresurrectable*. The depth of your disobedience does not matter, nor does the intensity of your rebellion. It matters not if you, like lucifer, have worshipped yourself and attempted to lift yourself higher than the One who made you. Your best idea can only take you high enough to die. Your best effort will only take you to the pinnacle of destruction, if you go alone. But even in your death and destruction, His life wind can fill you with a brand new Spirit, and you can live again.

As well, I saw amazing possibilities for the second man. I understood the circumstances of his life had left him bitter, confused and angry. It was not his fault. What is a child supposed to do but become an embittered adult if his father chooses self-gratification over the child and his mother? What is one to expect of a young child who is sexually harmed by a trusted adult, except he should act on his inner turmoil? The second man worshipped the tree because he could not embrace the idea of a loving father who makes magnificent trees but cherishes them much less than the man. But I saw hope and possibility for this man as well. I saw other compassionate, obedient men come to the tree and begin to massage balm into the dead man's feet and hands. Slowly, life and color began to inch their way up his limbs. Little by little he came alive as the balm worked its healing power. It occurred to me that the men had anointed the hanging brother with compassion and friendship. They bathed him with encouragement and hope. They healed him with the love of true fathers and brothers. They revealed to him the truth that had been hidden and the promise that had been buried. Ultimately, his possibility was complete restoration to the life his Creator originally intended. With strength he could not claim as his own, he could hoist himself enough to loosen his noose and descend from his own destruction. He could fall into the arms of his waiting brothers. It was his possibility to run with his new family into the neighboring Garden and shout and dance like a crazy man. Also, I understood the man could not come down from the tree and run to his freedom unless he did it himself. He had to want it! He had to reach up and take hold of the constriction shutting off his life flow. His brothers could only accomplish what they were purposed to do They could only count their obedience as legitimate if they were obedient to the command of the One who made them, for to do it any other way would amount to self-gratification. They were called only to be compassionate friends who came consistently bearing the balm of love and hope.

The Refugee
You dwelt in a place of disgust and disgrace
A land of carnage and pain
You lay in a pit, covered in your own vomit
And begged for the answer in vain
'Til at risk of derision, void of conscious decision
You reached for anonymous hand
Lending ear to the hark calling you from the dark
To the treasures of your Father's land
You shook from the cold and the venomous hold
That the bottle and pipe had supplied
'Til at last with a tear washing over your fear
You wished as a child you had died
But a flicker of light summoned you from the night

And you stumbled toward it to see
If the Lord of the house would his angels arouse
To take you in their company
But you fractured once more, crashing onto the floor
Of the valley of shadows and death
And you looked for the light that would splinter the night
Finding only dry bones without breath
And your mind felt alone, and your heart was a stone
And you thought this is how it must end
When the call came once more, nearer now than before
And it carried the tone of a friend
Then out of the dust with a smile you could trust
He came with a plate and a spoon
And he gave you a place at the table of grace
And he doctored your tiniest wound
And he stood by your side as a comfort and guide
And he brought his brothers along
And they lifted you high like a praise to the sky
And they're singing you out like a song
And they carry you still with a purpose and will
Toward the Father's bright hall
Where a robe and a ring He will joyfully bring
And will give you the keys to it all
So look not to the sky or the angels to fly
But look to your left and your right
For your brothers are there and they'll carry your care
THIS IS THE FATHER'S DELIGHT
And you'll surely grow strong as you travel along
And a brother you'll also become
And you'll help one or two just like they did for you
And together we'll all journey home

Days, weeks and months passed in my own journey, but the wind continued to blow. I remained very busy with the tasks associated with caring and providing for a large family and working for a thriving inner-city ministry, but the prayer was not lost in the hustle-bustle of life's activities. Rather, it became as steady as breath. The wind of revelation has not always blown violently, or even with recognizable force. Often, it has presented itself as a slight, steady breeze, but present nonetheless. My ears have not always been fully open and keen to the words of the revelation. They sometimes get clogged by the clamoring of so many voices or stopped up by polluted winds blowing from the direction of the graveyard. My eyes have not always been fully clear and focused, able to see the images sent to me on the winds of revelation. Sometimes stress and fatigue produce a film which blurs the vision. My mind and heart have not always been clean enough to receive and house the words and pictures revealed by the Spirit. They are occasionally fouled by refuse I allow to be dumped there.

The wind has continued to blow, at times with tornadic ferocity and at other times ever so slightly. I have been duly involved in the mundaneness of everyday living, such as pumping gas, cutting grass or answering an email, and have felt the caress of a Spirit breeze on my neck. I have awakened at very early hours and gone to my front porch, where I heard the haunting call of a leftover whippoorwill, the crow of a rooster on the neighbor's farm, and felt a steady breeze of revelation. I have traveled to another country and sat on a hillside overlooking God's idea of tropical paradise, and found the wind had followed me there.

Everywhere I look, I see rotting corpses, but always with melodies from a neighboring Garden blowing over them. There is HOPE! At this moment, I am compelled again to pray for my friend and his family. They are in trouble. My friend's eyes are clouded, his ears clogged and his heart and mind polluted. He has become willing to sacrifice his wife and children in order to worship himself. He is bowing at the foot of the tree of self-gratification. The noose will soon drop and he will hang in a death salute to his best idea.

But there is hope for him and there is hope for you. He is a symbol for all who will receive this prayer and make a decision for the graveyard or the Garden. As well, I am praying for those who read these words, whose Hope is buried under the rubble of disobedience, that the wind will blow away the fog that prevents them from seeing the Garden just next door to where they presently are. The prayer is not confined or stationary. It is woven into the stories and reflections found on these pages, and goes out from here in the spirits of those who embrace it. It is found in the contrasts between winners and losers and in the grievous paradox between the Father's original intention for His children and the confused condition in which we find ourselves. I cannot limit the prayer by consolidating it to one or two pages; it is much bigger than that. It manifests itself in the human experience through precious sons and daughters like Vanessa and Greg. Their lives preach that Hope remains for those who walk in obedience and that the Garden is a really cool place to live. It is revealed in people like Russell who continue to take baby steps toward the Garden's gates while serpents line up to whisper their lies, and presents the reality that "long obedience" in the same direction, as long as it is the Father's direction, indeed produces something worth living for. The prayer serves as a powerful teacher in the lives of Shawn and so many others who were not willing to "forsake all" and ultimately lost their battles. Only the father can judge them in death, but the rest of us can learn from their lives.

I just finished mile three and have been reminded of something I learned years ago, but that demands re-acquaintance each year. It is that an early September morning in central Georgia can quickly evolve from a pleasant reprieve from the previous month's "dog days" to a muggy reminder that summer has not yet released her grip. There is an enormous difference between 8:30 and 9:00, enough to change thoughts and alter language, but *there are no quitters* remains my mantra. I *will* finish the course. I will *not* allow this uphill grade to steal my victory. I *refuse* to submit to lactic acid and eyes that burn from salty sweat. I will *not* give in to humidity that makes me feel like I am breathing through a pillow case. There are all kinds of distractions but I cannot allow my mind to give residency to them or they will become gods that tell me where to go and what to do.

Once I was running on a matchless December afternoon, with temperature in the 40s and air as crisp as spring water, when I noticed a cloud on the western horizon that contrasted everything else about the day. It was not large and posed no real threat but its presence marred an otherwise pristine environment. It was very dark and ugly and seemed to have popped up out of nowhere. For a few moments, I forgot about the spectacular blue sky and cottony clouds that surrounded it on all sides. My mind drifted from the ideal temperature for running and the crisp cleanness of the air and I lost track of everything beautiful around me and focused on the one dark cloud. I began to recall pictures I saw on television of Hurricane Katrina's ominous black clouds rolling up over the Gulf and unleashing their fury. I thought of the resulting death and destruction and suddenly I felt tired and didn't want to run any more. I had to renew my strength by regaining focus and adjusting my course. I turned my back on the cloud and ran away from it and began to thank the Father for the amazing day and for the strength to get out and enjoy it. The following day I wrote this poem:

One Dark Cloud

One dark cloud, a lonely sullen mar
Against a sea of blue and puffy white
So vast the span of promise, so limitless the solace
So pregnant with Hope's expected child
But eyes refuse the glory and revel melancholy
Conversely on the black and evil fellow
Who from his pauperish prison, demanding all affection
Redeeming sorrow's penchant for the night
Consumes the heaven's bounty
Changing history's story
Revealing tragic duty
For all who crown as lord the one dark cloud

Miles four and five are torturous. I wish I could say I have entered runner's paradise and can no longer feel the throbbing in my right knee or the nagging Plantar Fasciitis in my heel, but I would be lying. Fact is I am a forty-nine year old man who is dying. I am living under a curse that began when my earliest ancestors disobeyed our Father and were expelled from their Garden home. I want the same chance they had. I want to know what it is really like to walk with our Father in the cool of the evening and have Him tell me great secrets and point out things to me that no man has ever seen. I want clarity of thought that never feels like I am looking through a screened door and clarity of hearing that easily distinguishes between His voice and the voices of whispering serpents. I want to move closer to Him each day; therefore, I must keep running because running breaks me down and makes me aware of His presence and opens my ears and eyes to His words and pictures.

Although distractions are there (dark clouds, squawking birds, ticking shoe laces, aching joints and cramping muscles, suffocating humidity and many, many more), I am consistently reminded that the run is symbolic of our Kingdom struggle and that I must remain obedient to it if I want to hear the Father's words and see His pictures. I am not insinuating every believer should be a runner. I know for some it is not even possible, but each of us should commit ourselves to something that stands as a symbol of our endeavor, something we can embrace and maintain a "long obedience" to that will serve as a rudder and keep us on course. Perhaps for you it is to regularly exercise a spiritual discipline, such as fasting. Perhaps you have a prayer life that always takes you to places of absolute intimacy where the

Father has your full attention. Maybe a different form of physical exercise is right for you, such as aerobics or Pilates. Whatever it is, I am confident the Father has things to share with us and He is waiting for our hearts and minds to be prepared to receive them. He wants us to move into the dwelling place He has prepared for us and live there in the fullness of His Peace, Power, Provision and Protection.

Mile six is finished and I am walking the "cool-down." This morning Father has shown me marvelous things and I can't wait to write them down. I am more convinced than ever that I can live in the fullness of all He created me to be. By the way, so can you.

The Gratification of the Run
It was when I turned…
thigh muscle screaming
heart threatening mortification
lungs twice collapsed and self-resuscitated
It was when I turned…
blister rising
knuckles clenched like fierce fighters
sweat drops racing like Indy cars on some bedeviled track
It was when I turned…
The evening sun making introductions
splashing my spirit like a fairy tale waterfall
the cool Georgia breeze massaging my soul
with strokes born of the hand of God
the redtail flapping, clapping his praise
nature's confirmation of something very, very good